Josephine Pollard

A Child's History of our Naval Heroes

Book 4

Josephine Pollard

A Child's History of our Naval Heroes
Book 4

ISBN/EAN: 9783348069885

Printed in Europe, USA, Canada, Australia, Japan

Cover: Foto ©ninafisch / pixelio.de

More available books at **www.hansebooks.com**

A CHILD'S HISTORY OF OUR NAVAL HEROS
Told In One-Syllable Words

I.—FIGHT BE-TWEEN THE MER-RI-MAC AND MON-I-TOR.

A CHILD'S HISTORY OF OUR NAVAL HEROES
Book 4
Illustrated

TOLD IN ONE-SYLLABLE WORDS

By Josephine Pollard
Published 1896

Published By
Mantle Ministries
228 Still Ridge, Bulverde, Texas 78163

BOYS and GIRLS:

WHO of you does not love to hear or to read sea-yarns spun by those who have been in dis-tant lands, and braved the dan-gers of the deep? We are thrilled through and through by tales of deeds done on ship-board, of hair-breadth es-capes, of wrecks and hard-ships borne by brave men iu Arc-tic Seas, and a-mong the ice-floes.

But when war is in the land and men have to be on guard a-gainst the foes that roam the high seas, then brave hearts are put to their great-est test, and we feel a pang of hor-ror as we read of the scenes of blood-shed through which they have passed.

In the year 1813, Cap-tain Law-rence, of the CHES-A-PEAKE, *was struck by a shot from the Brit-ish ship* SHAN-NON, *and fell dy-ing on the deck. His last or-der was "Don't give up the ship!" and this has been, since that time, the mot-to of the A-mer-i-can sail-or.*

Stick to the ship! Stand by your colors!

Do your du-ty where du-ty calls you: and let no man be more of a he-ro than you are when the time comes for you to act your part.

"Act WELL your part; there all the hon-or lies."

CONTENTS.

Chapter I.	MEN OF WAR	5
Chapter II.	HERE AND THERE ON THE COAST	21
Chapter III.	BLOCKADE RUNNERS	35
Chapter IV.	THE BATTLE OF PORT ROYAL	42
Chapter V.	THE MONITOR AND THE MERRIMAC	58
Chapter VI.	DAVID G. FARRAGUT	78
Chapter VII.	ON THE MISSISSIPPI	88
Chapter VIII.	OFF NEW ORLEANS AND VICKSBURG	103
Chapter IX.	UP THE RED RIVER	121
Chapter X.	BEFORE MOBILE	146
Chapter XI.	A YOUNG HERO	165
Chapter XII.	THE ATTACK ON FORT FISHER	180
Appendix.	NAVAL HEROES OF THE WAR WITH SPAIN	193

OUR NAVAL HEROES.

CHAPTER I.

MEN-OF-WAR.

An in-land na-tion has no need of boats to de-fend it-self from the at-tacks of foes. Its pride and its strength lie in its ar-my of strong, staunch men, who go forth to bat-tle, and to do the will of those in com-mand.

A na-tion that lies on the sea-coast has a long line of ports, or doors, through which a foe could make his way, and has need of a na-vy, of men-of-war, and of armed vessels, as well as mer-chant ships to trade in dis-tant lands.

Then, of course, there must be schools in which to train men and boys to serve on ship-board; and these schools are known as na-val a-cad-e-mies. The first one in France was built a-bout the year 1630, and Eng-land did not have one un-til 100 years la-ter.

The first na-val school in the U-ni-ted States was found-ed at An-nap-o-lis, Ma-ry-land, in the year 1845, and was con-duct-ed on much the same plan as the school for the ar-my at West Point.

School-ships were not heard of un-til the year 1874, so that up to that time boys had not much chance to learn what life on board a man-of-war was like, though they might know the rules of war by heart. The rules on board these school-ships have to be quite strict, as bad boys some-times get on board, and would play all sorts of pranks, if they were not held in check with strong reins.

These school-ships sail all round the world, and the boys on board of them see strange sights, and learn a great deal that they will not find in books, and can-not be taught at home.

The first les-son they have to learn is a hard one for most boys; and that is—TO O-BEY—AT ONCE.

They must know all a-bout the ship, how it is made, and what each part of it is called, so that they can give things their right names. They must know how to reef and furl a sail; how to splice the ropes and to make all sorts of knots; how to load and fire a can-non; how to use a swab; how to keep things neat and snug; how to sleep in a ham-mock; and a host of queer things that some boys would not care to know. It used to be quite

FURL-ING SAIL.

the style for boys to run off to sea when things did not please them at home. If they thought they could loll on deck, and take their ease, play tricks and do just as they liked, they soon found out their mis-take, when they got on ship-board, and oh! how some of them longed for the nice bed, the good food, and the kind friends to whom they were so glad to say good-by! Some were too proud to let their hard-ships be known, and ate salt junk and hard-tack, and forced them-selves to make a show as if they were fond of such fare.

Some boys watched for a chance, and ran back to the homes which they had learned to prize, and proved by

SCHOOL-SHIP FOR BOYS.

this act that they were not born to be he-roes. But for some, life on ship-board has a great charm, and they are nev-er so much at home and at ease as when they are on the deep blue sea.

It costs a great deal to keep up an ar-my and a na-vy, and as the U-ni-ted States had had no use for ships of war for near-ly 50 years, they had not thought it worth while to build new ves-sels that would rot in their docks, or to keep on hand a large stock of na-val stores.

The in-crease of com-merce and of trav-el had caused an im-mense num-ber of ships to be built, which were owned by pri-vate par-ties or stock com-pa-nies, and not by the U-ni-ted States gov-ern-ment.

But there is a prov-erb that says, "in times of peace pre-pare for war," and those wise words were brought home to the loy-al part of the U-ni-ted States at the out-break of the civ-il war. Ri-fle-guns, rams, and tor-pe-does were un-known, and most of the ships owned by the gov-ern-ment were then cruis-ing far from the home ports.

The sail-ing frig-ate SA-BINE, 50 guns, the sail-ing sloop ST. LOU-IS, 20, and the steam-er BROOK-LYN, 25, and WY-AN-DOT-TE, 5, were at Pen-sa-co-la; and the sail-ing ves-sels MAC-E-DO-NI-AN, 24 guns, the CUM-BER-LAND 24, and the steam-ers POC-A-HON-TAS 5, and POW-HAT-AN, 11, were on their way from Ve-ra Cruz.

On the coast of Af-ri-ca were the sail-ing sloops CON-STEL-LA-TION and PORTS-MOUTH, 22 guns each, the store-ship RE-LIEF, 2 guns, and the steam-ers MO-HI-CAN 6, MYS-TIC, 5, SUM-TER, 5, and SAN JA-CIN-TO, 13. The steam frig-ate NI-AG-A-RA, 20, was on its way from Ja-pan, and ar-rived at Bos-ton, Ap-ril 20th, 1861.

In the na-vy yards at the north were the steam frig-ates WA-BASH, MIN-NE-SO-TA, COL-O-RA-DO, and RO-AN-OKE, of 4 guns each. These were put in as good or-der as pos-si-ble and sent out to do duty a-long the coast.

Of the nine-ty ves-sels that the gov-ern-ment owned in 1861, fif-ty were of the old style—ships-of-the-line, frig-ates, sloops, and brigs—and some of these were still on the stocks. Some had been fine ships in their day, but their day was past.

Of the for-ty steam-ers in the list, five were un-fit for use, two of them be-ing still in the stocks, and the rest good for noth-ing but re-ceiv-ing ships. Two more were mere tugs. Eight oth-ers, and a-mong them were the five frig-ates, were laid up, as there had been up to this time no need of their ser-vi-ces.

ON THE STOCKS.

Not on-ly were the ships old and un-fit to take part in a great war, but the of-fi-cers on board of them were old al-so, and too set in their old ways to try new ones, and there were but 5,000 men in the na-vy, where there was need of at least 50,000.

Long years of peace had made the na-tion care-less, but as soon as it a-woke to the fact that "a man's worst foes are those of his own house-hold," there was a stir that shook A-mer-i-ca in all its length and breadth.

The North went to work at once and bought up all sorts of ves-sels, from screw-steam-ers and side-wheel-ers of 2,000 tons, to fer-ry-boats, and tugs of light weight.

Some of the large steam-ers were fast sail-ers and made first-rate cruis-ers. The CON-NECT-I-CUT, the CUY-LER, and the SAN-TI-A-GO DE CU-BA more than paid for their cost in the pri-zes they took. The steam-er CIR-CAS-SIAN, one of the most val-u-a-ble pri-zes of the war was seized by a Ful-ton fer-ry-boat. The fer-ry-boats that ply in the North and East riv-ers are very strong-ly built, and their heav-y guns made them a force by no means to be des-pised.

FER-RY BOAT.

The first thing

the North did was to *buy* ves-sels; the next thing was to *build*; and by the last of the year eight brand new sloops-of-war were set a-float. Four of these, the O-nei-da, Kear-sarge, Wa-chu-sett, and Tus-ca-ro-ra, were made af-ter old plans, so that the work went on with more speed, than if they had had to wait for new ones to be drawn.

The next move of the Na-vy De-part-ment was to have ves-sels made by men who had ship-yards of their own, and in this way 23 small heav-i-ly armed screw gun-boats, were built. Some of them in four months from the time the con-tract was made, were a-float, armed and manned, and took part in the bat-tle of Port Roy-al. From the haste in which they were built they were known as the "nine-ty day gun-boats," and were of great use to the na-vy in bat-tles and block-ades.

For use in the riv-ers, nar-row sounds, and chan-nels, there was need of small ves-sels of light draught, and to save the trou-ble of turn-ing a-round they were built with a bow and a rud-der at each end.

Some of the large ves-sels that cost more than 1,000-000 dol-lars made but one cruise. They were built of white-oak in-stead of live-oak, of which it was the cus-tom to make ships-of-war, and as soon as they were

DOUB-LE END-ER.

launched on the wa-ter they be-gan to de-cay, and were in too rot-ten a state to be re-paired.

The next thing was to build i-ron-clads; and by the end of the year the U-ni-ted States na-vy had a large fleet of ships of all sorts and si-zes:—steam-boats, rams, tin-clads, mer-chant-men, mor-tar-boats, sloops, gun-boats, and fer-ry-boats, all in charge of a-ble com-mand-ers who did he-ro-ic ser-vice du-ring the war.

Gen-er-al Dix, who was Sec-re-ta-ry of the Treas-u-ry, heard that the reb-els were a-bout to seize the rev-e-nue cut-ters that were at Mo-bile and at New Or-le-ans, and he sent a man down to se-cure them. He was too late for the one at Mo-bile, and when he reached New Or-le-ans he found that Bresh-wood, the com-mand-er of the McCLEL-LAND, had gone with the South, and would not give up the boat.

This word was at once sent to Dix, by tel-e-graph,

and he sent back an or-der for the ar-rest of Breshwood, in which were these words:

"IF AN-Y ONE AT-TEMPTS TO HAUL DOWN THE A-MER-I-CAN FLAG, SHOOT HIM ON THE SPOT;" and ev-er since they have seemed a part of the A-mer-i-can flag, wov-en in with the red, white, and blue.

The mid-ship-men at the Na-val schools were mere boys who had not yet served their full term; but the need of of-fi-cers was so great, that these lads had to be brought to the front, and put in pla-ces of great trust. They did their du-ty well, and some of the most he-ro-ic deeds of the war were done by these brave boys who felt no fear, and went in-to bat-tle with light hearts and bright eyes, and the won-der-ful pluck that seems to be-long to Young A-mer-i-ca. There was great need of well-trained sea-men, but as these could not be had on short no-tice, the ships had to be manned with such as came in an-swer to a call for vol-un-teers. Some of these had been on mer-chant ves-sels, or had served as pi-lots; some had nev-er been to sea at all; and but few of them knew how to han-dle such guns as are used on men-of-war. But what they lacked in skill, they made up in brav-er-y, and as they were quick to learn they did them-selves great cred-it, and de-serve to share in the fame that was won by our na-val he-roes in the great re-bell-ion.

When the war broke out the Na-val school at An-nap-o-lis was closed, and the young men sent to the school at New-port, Rhode Isl-(*ile*) and.

Up to this time the South had not one ship of war. Why was this? Well, in the first place she had had no need of ves-sels of that class.

None of the men of the South had been trained to fol-low the sea. She had two ship-yards, three roll-ing mills, and a few ma-chine shops, but at none of these could such work be done as there was need of, and the one found-ry where big guns could be cast was kept go-ing night and day.

In the month of March, a large sum had been got to-geth-er with which to buy or make ten steam-gun-boats. The steam-bat-ter-y FUL-TON had been seized at Pen-sa-co-la, and much mon-ey was spent to put her in war trim, and by dint of ma-king use of all it could lay hands on, the South made out to get up quite a small fleet, though it hard-ly de-served to be called a na-vy.

But this was the work of months, and we must go

back now to see what took place in the mean-time, and what need there was of haste and skill on the part of those who sought to save the U-ni-on.

At the North, it was thought that Wash-ing-ton would be seized at once by the reb-els, un-less something was done to pre-vent it. So the ar-my and na-vy were called to de-fend her, and in a short time her streets and av-e-nues were filled with troops, quick to ral-ly round the flag, and she be-came the most mil-i-ta-ry cit-y on the con-ti-nent.

While the thoughts of the North were on Wash-ing-ton, and the need of send-ing troops there, the reb-els were do-ing great harm by seiz-ing some of the most im-por-tant pla-ces in-land and on the coast.

It was a great blow to the North when the Na-vy yard at Nor-folk, Vir-gin-i-a, fell in-to reb-el hands. It was the chief na-val sta-tion of the U-ni-ted States, at which the lar-gest ships could en-ter, and had, be-sides. a hos-pi-tal and dry-dock, both of which would be of great use in time of war. The ves-sels of war there at that time were the Ships of the Line:—PENN-SYL-VA-NI-A, 120 guns; CO-LUM-BUS, 80; DEL-A-WARE, 84; NEW YORK, 84. Frig-ates:—U-NI-TED STATES, 50 guns; CO-LUM-BUS, 50; RAR-I-TAN, 50. Sloops of War:—PLY-MOUTH, 22 guns; GER-MAN-TOWN, 22. Brig:—DOL-PHIN, 4 guns. Steam frig-ate, MER-RI-MAC, 40 guns.

All of these were not in first-rate or-der, but re-pairs could at once have been made, and the ves-sels, old and new, sent where they could have been of most use to the Gov-ern-ment that owned them. But in the first shock of great con-flicts mob rule has sway, and men wild with drink, or with rage for which there is no ex-cuse, do strange deeds, and com-mit all sorts of crimes, un-til the law comes in to re-strain them. This was the case both North and South; each felt there was no time to lose, and pri-zes to be ta-ken must be seized at once. De-lays were dan-ger-ous.

Some reb-els with-out wait-ing for or-ders seized all the light boats in the Nor-folk Na-vy yard, and sunk them at the mouth of the har-bor, so that the large ves-sels of war could not be ta-ken a-way.

At this time the Na-vy yard was in charge of U-ni-on men, and still un-der con-trol of the Gov-ern-ment of the U-ni-ted States. When word reached Nor-folk that the CUM-BER-LAND was a-bout to sail, it caused a great stir in that cit-y, which was large-ly filled with reb-els, and plans were laid to pre-vent her.

At noon, on the 20th of A-pril, an of-fi-cer went from

SINK-ING VES-SELS.

the yard with a flag of truce, and made his way to the head-quar-ters of the reb-el gen-er-al in com-mand of the troops at Nor-folk. The two had a long talk to-geth-er, and the com-man-dant of the yard was forced to give his word that none of the ves-sels should be re-moved, nor a shot fired ex-cept in self-de-fence.

This made things more qui-et for a-while; but as soon as it was learned that the GER-MAN-TOWN and MER-RI-MAC had been scut-tled, and that the men at the yard were throw-ing o-ver-board small arms and side arms, and de-stroy-ing much that was of val-ue, the storm of hate raged more fierce-ly on the "sa-cred soil of Vir-gin-i-a." South-ern of-fi-cers on du-ty at the yard re-signed, or de-sert-ed.

At mid-night a fire was start-ed in the Na-vy yard, and be-fore day-light the ship-hou-ses, and some of the ves-sels of war moored near the edge of the chan-nel were in a blaze. The scene was a grand one. The roar of the flames could be heard for miles and miles; and, as they felt the heat, the great guns of the PENN-SYL-VA-NI-A, one af-ter the oth-er, sent forth their shot with loud re-ports that seemed to shake earth, sea, and sky.

The PAW-NEE, which had just come back from a cruise left Wash-ing-ton on the 18th, and reached For-tress Mon-roe on the af-ter-noon of the next day. Here she took on board some troops, and two hours la-ter came in sight of Nor-folk. The CUM-BER-LAND and PENN-SYL-VA-NI-A were ly-ing off the yard, and the men on board, think-ing the PAW-NEE was a foe, be-gan to get their guns read-y to fire on her. The wind blew so that the voi-ces of those on the PAW-NEE, could not be heard by those near-er shore. An of-fi-cer on board the PENN-SYL-VA-NI-A thought of this, and he asked the com-man-dant of that ves-sel to cheer the stran-ger. This was done, and the PAW-NEE was saved, and at once came to the re-lief of her sis-ter ships. She took the CUM-BER-LAND in tow, and left her at an-chor down the har-bor, out of the reach of dan-ger, with the Com-man-dant of the yard, Com-mo-dore McCau-ley, and oth-er of-fi-cers on board, and a large sup-ply of mil-i-ta-ry stores.

The Com-mo-dore at first re-fused to leave his post, and an of-fi-cer had to be sent to bring him off. Though much was burnt up that was of val-ue, the work was done in such haste, by the loy-al men, that a great deal was left un-harmed, and, of course, fell in-to the hands of their foes. There were tons and tons of pow-der, great num-bers of load-ed shells, and at least two thou-sand great guns, three hun-dred of which were quite new, and had cost a large sum of mon-ey.

The loss was a se-vere one; and what made it ten times worse was, that the North had put in-to the hands of her foes, all these war weap-ons which would be used a-gainst her, and which were such a great gain to the South.

CHAPTER II.

HERE AND THERE ON THE COAST.

WAR was de-clared when sev-en South-ern States vo-ted them-selves out of the U-ni-on. All the forts, ar-se-nals, dock-yards, cus-tom hou-ses, rev-e-nue cut-ters, and all the na-val and mil-i-ta-ry stores in these States, were held by per-sons who thought they were do-ing what was right and just.

Forts Pick-ens, Tay-lor, and Jef-fer-son, near the Flor-i-da coast, and Sum-ter in Charles-ton har-bor, were the on-ly ones that re-mained un-der the flag of the U-ni-on.

Fort Sum-ter was the larg-est of the forts in Charles-ton har-bor. It was well-built, oc-ta-gon in shape, and had on three sides two rows of port-holes for heav-y guns. On the south, or land side, it had loop-holes for mus-kets, as well as o-pen-ings for big guns; and the wharf on this side could be swept by a cross-fire, from all the loop-holes and port-holes fa-cing that way.

At noon, on the 27th of De-cem-ber, 1860, the Stars and Stripes were hoist-ed o-ver the fort, and Charles-ton knew that Ma-jor An-der-son was in pos-ses-si-on. He had with him but a hand-ful of men, and as it be-came known that the reb-els meant to at-tack Sum-ter, it was de-cid-ed to send the wo-men and chil-dren from the fort. They were ta-ken to Charles-ton, and placed on board the steam-er Ma-ri-on, bound to New York. She left on Sun-day, Feb-ru-a-ry 3, with the wives and chil-dren of the of-fi-cers in the fort, and as she drew near Sum-ter a strange and thrill-ing scene took place.

The whole gar-ri-son stood on top of the ram-parts, and when the ship was pass-ing fired a gun, and gave three heart-break-ing cheers, as a fare-well to the loved ones, whom they might nev-er meet a-gain this side the grave. Those on board the Ma-ri-on wept, and waved

DE-PART-URE OF THE MA-RI-ON.

fare-wells to hus-bands and fa-thers—a small, brave band shut up in a lone-ly fort in the midst of cru-el foes. Five forts could be seen from the steam-er's deck with their guns point-ed at Sum-ter.

It was at half past four o'clock on the morn-ing of A-pril 12, 1861, that the first gun was fired, the ech-o of which rang through all the States—once so u-ni-ted—and made stout hearts quake with fear. For this war was like no oth-er war that had ev-er ta-ken place.

Shot and shell poured forth their dead-ly fire from the fort on James' Isl-and. Then Fort Moul-trie joined in, and soon the guns from all the points a-round sent forth their wrath at the grim fort, that dared to hold a-loft the Stars and Stripes, and seemed to frown up-on its foes. All through the day and night the fi-ring was kept up, and some of the guns sent hot shot, which fell on the roof of the of-fi-cers' quar-ters, and they were soon in flames. The wind blew from the south, and bore the flames to the roof of the bar-racks, and by twelve o'clock all the wood-work on that side of the fort was in a blaze. The men had to work hard to keep the pow-der mag-a-zine from ex-plo-ding, and a large num-ber of bar-rels full of pow-der had to be thrown in-to the sea.

Clouds of smoke-cin-ders blown through the case-

THE BAR-RACKS ON FIRE.

mates, by the wind, set on fire box-es, beds, and oth-er things be-long-ing to the men, and made it un-safe for them to keep the small stock of pow-der they were in such great need of.

They had so few cart-ridg-es left that they did not dare to waste them, and guns were fired but six times an hour. Mean-while the foe kept up their storm of i-ron hail. Bul-lets hissed through the air like fi-e-ry ser-pents. Can-nons boomed. Some-times a shell would burst in mid-air right o-ver the doomed fort-ress, and all a-round were flash-es of flame that seemed to come from de-mon eyes. The night was pitch dark, and made a fine back-ground for so weird a scene, and as shot and shell sped on their way each marked its course by a long trail of fire that flashed and fa-ded in a mo-ment.

When the flames were at their height, word was brought to Ma-jor An-der-son that Mr. Wig-fall, with a white flag, was out-side Fort Sum-ter and wished to speak to him. The Ma-jor went out to meet the reb-el of-fi-cer, pass-ing un-der the bla-zing gate-way. In the mean-time Wig-fall had gone to an o-pen-ing on the left flank, where, by show-ing the white flag on his sword, he was al-lowed to en-ter.

Wig-fall said to the of-fi-cers that he came from Gen-er-al Beau-re-gard to ask that the fight should cease for a-while. As the flag of the fort had been shot down, the fire was ra-ging, and the gar-ri-son (the troops in the fort) were in a great strait, it was best for them to hoist the white flag.

He was told that the Stars and Stripes still waved from the par-a-pet, and that the white flag would not be hoist-ed ex-cept by or-der of the com-mand-ing of-fi-cer. They told Mr. Wig-fall that his own bat-ter-ies should first cease fi-ring. The one on Cum-mings Point, from which he came, had done so, and he asked that his own white flag might be waved as a sign that those on Sul-li-van's Isl-and should cease al-so.

This was re-fused; but he was told that he might wave the white flag him-self, if he chose, and he got up in one of the deep win-dows—or em-bra-sures, as they are called—for that pur-pose. He did this for a few mo-ments, and then a cor-po-ral was sent to take his place. Soon, how-ev-er, a shot struck quite near the o-pen-ing, and the cor-po-ral jumped in-side and de-clared to Mr. Wig-fall that "he would not hold his flag, for it was not re-spect-ed."

By this time Ma-jor An-der-son came up, and Wig-fall re-peat-ed what he had said to the oth-er of-fi-cers, praised him for the brave de-fence he had made, and asked that the war-fare should cease so that terms could be ar-ranged.

An-der-son asked what terms he came to of-fer. "Any terms you de-sire," said Wig-fall. "Your own terms—the na-ture of which, Gen. Beau-re-gard will ar-range with you."

An-der-son said that he would ac-cept the terms pro-posed by Beau-re-gard on the 11th; which were that he was to leave the fort with his com-mand, ta-king arms and all the goods they owned, sa-lu-ting the U-ni-ted States flag as it was ta-ken down, and be-ing borne to an-y North-ern port that he might de-sire.

Then Mr. Wig-fall left, the white flag was raised, and the Stars and Stripes low-ered, by or-der of the com-mand-ing of-fi-cer. Soon af-ter this was done a boat came from Charles-ton in which were three aides of Gen-er-al Beau-re-gard with a mes-sage for Ma-jor An-der-son. Beau-re-gard had seen the white flag hoist-ed, and sent to know what aid he could lend in put-ting out the flames. Be-ing told of the state of af-fairs, and of Mr. Wig-fall's vis-it, these men said that al-though in com-mand of a part of Beau-re-gard's troops, Wig-fall had not seen the Gen-er-al for two days.

THE WHITE FLAG.

Hear-ing this, the com-man-dant said that the U-ni-ted States flag would be raised a-gain at once, but the reb-el aides begged him to wait un-til they had time to see their chief and learn his wish-es.

They soon came back with word that Beau-re-gard would ac-cept all the terms but the one that re-ferred to the flag. Af-ter-wards he gave his con-sent that the Stars and Stripes should be hon-ored by those who still held dear the one true flag.

On Sun-day af-ter-noon, A-pril 14, An-der-son and his men marched out of the fort with col-ors fly-ing, and drums beat-ing, and a sa-lute of fif-ty guns was fired in hon-or of the flag which had been forced to give way to that which bore the "South-ern Cross."

SA-LU-TING THE FLAG.

The news of the fall of Fort Sum-ter spread far and wide, and then came Lin-coln's call "to arms! to arms!" which sent an e-lec-tric thrill through the peo-ple, North and South.

The Sec-re-ta-ry of War called on all the States to fur-nish troops, and the way in which the re-quest was re-ceived by the lead-ing men will show you the state of feel-ing at that time.

The Gov-ern-or of Ken-tuck-y said: "Ken-tuck-y

will fur-nish no troops for the wick-ed pur-pose of sub-du-ing her sis-ter South-ern States."

The Gov-ern-or of North Car-o-li-na said: "You can get no troops from North Car-o-li-na."

The Gov-ern-or of Vir-gin-i-a said: "The troops of Vir-gin-i-a will not be fur-nish-ed to the pow-ers at Wash-ing-ton for an-y such use or pur-pose as they have in view."

The Gov-ern-or of Ten-nes-see said: "Ten-nes-see will not fur-nish a sin-gle man for co-er-cion,"—that is, to put down the South—"but fif-ty thou-sand, if nec-es-sa-ry, for de-fence of our rights, or those of our South-ern broth-ers."

The Gov-ern-or of Mis-sou-ri said that the re-quest was "il-le-gal, in-hu-man, and di-a-bol-i-cal, and could not be com-plied with."

The Gov-ern-or of Rhode Isl-and of-fered the ser-vi-ces of in-fant-ry and ar-til-ler-y.

The Gov-ern-or of Mas-sa-chu-setts or-dered troops out *at once*, and in fif-ty hours three reg-i-ments from that State were on their way to Wash-ing-ton.

Con-nect-i-cut, New York, New Jer-sey, Penn-syl-va-ni-a, and all the North-ern States were prompt to of-fer arms, mon-ey, men, and rail-roads; and at the wharves in New York, were steam-ers wait-ing to con-vey the large num-bers of troops, that were mo-ving to-ward the de-fence of the Cap-i-tol of the U-ni-ted States.

The strife, which it was thought would end in a few days, was kept up, and the news of bat-tles lost and won, fed the flame that each day gained in force and fu-ry.

A-mong the troops that left New York, were reg-i-ments that went by the name of "Zou-aves." They were made up of strong and brave men, full of nerve and dash, and were led by of-fi-cers as bold and fear-less. They were drest in a strange garb—half Turk-ish and half A-rab—with wide bag-gy trou-sers of red flan-nel, white belts, and white leg-gings, and a red fez cap.

This gay dress was sure to draw crowds when the reg-i-ment, or e-ven a small part of it, was seen on the streets, and brave deeds were ex-pect-ed of men in such brave at-tire. One of these reg-i-ments went by the name of "Bil-ly Wil-son's Zou-aves," and was made up of rough boys and men, some of whom were looked up-on, e-ven by their mates, as pret-ty hard ca-ses. These were a-mong the first to of-fer their ser-vi-ces to the Pres-i-dent when he sent out his first call for troops, and for their country's good they were sent to the Gulf of

Mexico to add to the strength of Fort Pick-ens, the on-ly fort that had not been seized by the reb-el foe.

They went in-to camp on San-ta Ro-sa Isl-and, near the fort, and kept guard on Pen-sa-co-la Bay; but though quite near the foe for some time, there were no fights be-tween the two, and no chance for the "Zou-aves" to show their skill and strength.

But ere long the chance came, and this story of them is told by a reb-el of-fi-cer who was an eye-wit-ness of the scene :

"Last night the foe per-formed the most brill-iant act which has yet marked the his-to-ry of the war. For some time past they have shown that they were ea-ger for a fight, and have grown more and more bold and da-ring. First they fired on one of our schoon-ers. Next, they burned the dry-dock; and last night, Sep-tem-ber 13, they made a most da-ring and reck-less raid on the na-vy yard. A-bout three o'clock in the morn-ing, five launch-es, with a-bout thir-ty men in each, pulled a-cross from San-ta Ro-sa Isl-and to the na-vy yard, a dis-tance of a-bout two miles. Each launch had in it a small brass how-itz-er on a piv-ot. (A how-itz-er is a small light can-non, that will send a large shell with on-ly a small cnarge of pow-der.)

"Their main ob-ject seems to have been to burn the lar-gest schoon-er of our har-bor po-lice, which was at anch-or, near the wharf. They were led by an of-fi-cer with the cour-age of for-ty Nu-mid-i-an li-ons, and their suc-cess was per-fect.

"Un-der cov-er of the dark-ness, si-lent-ly, and with muf-fled oars, they crept to-ward the wharf, and were not seen un-til quite near it. They then pulled with all speed to the schoon-er, and hooked fast to her, when their dar-ing lead-er shout-ed 'Board her!' lead-ing the way him-self with a cut-lass in one hand, and a bla-zing fire-ball in the oth-er.

"He threw the flam-ing torch in-to the hold of the schoon-er, and feel-ing sure that she was on fire, he or-dered his men to take to their launch-es and pull for life, as he said that a show-er of grape-shot would soon be rat-tling af-ter them.

"They pulled off a short dis-tance; but be-fore go-ing, they sent a show-er of grape from their how-itz-ers up-on our men as they were form-ing. The dark-ness made the fire un-cer-tain and on-ly two of our men were wound-ed.

"The schoon-er burned rap-id-ly, and we had to cut her loose from the wharf to save that from de-struc-tion. She float-ed off on the tide, send-ing forth a bright flood of light o-ver the sur-round-ing dark-ness of the scene."

The "Zou-aves" won the name of be-ing the most dar-ing and reck-less troops that took part in the war, but as they fought most-ly on land we will turn from the deeds of these "wild A-rabs"—some of them were lit-tle else—and give heed to the boys in jack-ets of blue.

As soon as the Nor-folk na-vy yard was in their hands, the reb-els went at once to put it in-to shape for their own use. Great grief was felt in Nor-folk o-ver the loss of the PENN-SYL-VA-NI-A, which had been for a long time a great or-na-ment to the har-bor, and had been one of the sights of the cit-y. They mourn-ed al-so that the new and hand-some frig-ate MER-RI-MAC, and four or five oth-er ves-sels had been giv-en to the flames or sunk in deep wa-ters.

It was not long, how-ev-er, be-fore word came to the North that the reb-els had raised the MER-RI-MAC, and were fit-ting her out in such a way, that it would be hard to find a ship to match her. There was not thought to be much truth in these tales, but still a sharp look-out was kept up, and the ships rode at anch-or with springs on their ca-bles, that would serve as a-larm bells to those who kept watch. The news proved to be most true.

The Mer-ri-mac was a frig-ate of 3,500 tons and 40 guns, and was more than 300 feet in length. Her cap-tors had her cut down to her old berth deck, and both ends, for 70 feet, were cov-ered o-ver so that the ves-sel was e-ven with the wa-ter. In the space be-tween—what is known as a-mid-ships—a slant-ing roof was built that was 24 inch-es thick, and sev-en feet a-bove the gun deck.

The prow was of cast i-ron four feet in length; the pi-lot house, which was in front of the smoke-stack, was cov-ered with i-ron four inch-es thick, and the sides of the ves-sel were pro-tect-ed in the same way. Both ends were round-ed so that by the use of piv-ot guns, she could be made a bow or a stern chas-er, and her name was changed to Vir-gin-i-a.

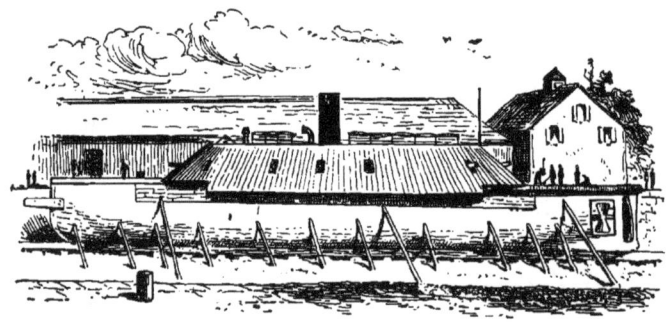

MER-RI-MAC, OR VIR-GIN-I-A.

There was no doubt of the strength of the big i-ron-clad, but there was one great thing that she lacked, and that was speed. She had al-ways been a slow boat, and on her last trip, her en-gines and boil-ers were found to be so weak, that no de-pend-ence could be placed on them.

Though the reb-els gave her the name of Vir-gin-i-a, the name of Mer-ri-mac still clung to her, and in her fight with the Mon-i-tor, which I will tell you a-bout by-and-by, she won great fame, and made it clear to all the world that na-val bat-tles should be fought with i-ron-clads.

CHAPTER III.

BLOCK-ADE RUN-NERS.

A GREAT deal of the trade of the South was with En-gland, and though Queen Vic-to-ri-a had made it known, that she would take no part in the war be-tween North and South, the trade was still kept up be-tween En-gland and South-ern ports. There was but one way to stop this, and that was to block-ade the ports; and there-fore, six days af-ter the fall of Fort Sum-ter, the

Pres-i-dent, A-bra-ham Lin-coln, gave or-ders that there should be a block-ade of the South-ern States, from South Car-o-li-na to Tex-as; and a few days la-ter the block-ade was stretched a-long the coast of Vir-gin-i-a, and North Car-o-li-na.

That on the At-lan-tic coast was called the North and South At-lan-tic Squad-ron. That in the Gulf of Mex-i-co was known as the East and West Gulf Squad-ron; and that which did serv-ice on the great riv-er, which is called "the fa-ther of all wa-ters," was known as the Mis-sis-sip-pi Flo-til-la

The terms of the block-ade were these: If a ves-sel tried to en-ter or leave a port with a view to break the block-ade, she was to be warned by one of the com-mand-ers of the block-a-ding fleet, who would put down the day and date, and the fact that such a boat had been du-ly warned. If the same boat tried the same thing a sec-ond time she would be seized at once, and ta-ken to a new port where there was a court of law to de-cide what should be done in the case. It may be well to state here that the deck of a ves-sel is—most of all in war times—a part of the soil of the na-tion whose flag she flies, and a fight with an En-glish or French ship means war with En-gland and France.

There are some isles in the At-lan-tic O-cean, on a line with North Car-o-li-na and Geor-gi-a, that be-long to En-gland, and at four points the trade was kept up with the South: Ber-mu-da, Nas-sau, Ha-van-a and Mat-a-mo-ras. Of these, Nas-sau was the chief. The chief seats of com-merce in the South, were Wil-ming-ton, Charles-ton and Sa-van-nah, and great bales of cotton stood on their wharves wait-ing to be ex-changed, for the car-goes that were on board the block-ade run-ners.

Some folks will find a way to break the laws, no matter how strict they may be made, or how great a risk they may run. The law was that both ship and car-go should be-come pri-zes if caught, in case the own-er knew, when his ship set out, that it was to en-ter, if it could, one of the block-a-ded ports. But it was of-ten the case, that the own-er did not know that his ves-sel was to take part in un-law-ful trade, as the bills of la-ding would be made out, and the ves-sel hired to take goods to Ber-mu-da or Nas-sau. Here the car-goes would be un-load-ed by con-fed-er-ate a-gents, and put on small-er boats that were in the hands of skill-ful pi-lots.

These boats, which were paint-ed a light lead col-or, would steal out when the nights were dark, show no

BLOCK-ADE RUN-NER.

lights, make no noise, and sneak a-long past the block-a-ding squad-ron, nor rouse those who kept guard un-der the U-ni-on flag. In this way they would run the block-ade o-ver and o-ver a-gain, with-out be-ing caught.

If caught at last, and tak-en to some near port to have the law de-cide the case, they would oft-times get free be-cause they bore no flag, and no sign that they were of En-glish birth. As the Queen had giv-en her word, that she would not take part with the North or the South, if her ships were found in our seas giv-ing aid to the foe, she might, by right of war, be seized as a prize, and En-gland would have to pay all the costs.

Quite a large num-ber of ves-sels had gone out from South-ern ports as pri-va-teers, and had al-read-y done much harm to the com-merce of the North. As some of these pri-va-teers had been seized, and their crews held as pris-on-ers, the reb-el Pres-i-dent, Jeff. Da-vis, made it known that he would grant *let-ters of marque* to his sub-jects. These let-ters of marque gave the men of the South pow-er to seize ves-sels that bore the Red-White-and-Blue flag, and to serve the crews as they chose, and to cruise as pi-rates of the high seas.

One of the first ves-sels that took out let-ters of marque, was the PE-TREL—once the rev-e-nue cut-ter AI-KEN, which fell in-to the hands of the reb-els when Fort Sum-ter was tak-en. Her crew had gone o-ver to the en-e-my, and were well fit-ted to wear false col-ors, and to do base deeds.

The PE-TREL ran the block-ade, but had no soon-er put to sea, than she fell in with the U-ni-ted States frig-ate ST. LAW-RENCE, and was seized.

The Cap-tain of the ST. LAW-RENCE saw the South-ern ves-sel in the dis-tance, and at once hauled down his heav-y spars and closed the port-holes. Then, with the men all be-low, the old frig-ate looked much like a large mer-chant ves-sel, and the pri-va-teer bore down on her think-ing to catch a rich prize.

The com-mand-er of the PE-TREL, gave the ST. LAW-

RENCE a round ball o-ver her bows, and some can-is-ter o-ver the stern, but the frig-ate sailed on as if try-ing to get a-way.

Then the PE-TREL gave chase, and when in range of the frig-ate the lat-ter o-pened her ports, and sent a fierce fire of shot and shell in-to the pri-va-teer. One of the round shot—a 32-pound-er—struck the PE-TREL a-mid-ships, and stove a hole in her be-low the wa-ter, so that she sank in a few mo-ments. Four of the crew were drowned, and the rest—thir-ty-six in num-ber—were saved.

So sud-den and sur-pris-ing was the at-tack of the St. Law-rence, that those on board the PE-TREL were quite dazed, and it is said that some of the men, when fished out of the wa-ter, were at a loss to know what had hap-pened to them.

Du-ring the year 1861, the reb-els had seized 58 North-ern ves-sels, some of them hav-ing rich car-goes, and their suc-cess in this line filled them with pride, and made them e-ven more bold and da-ring.

The old style of block-ade was to have the ves-sels cruise a-long the coast, and keep a sharp look-out for the block-ade run-ners. But the At-lan-tic and Gulf coasts were so bro-ken with bays and riv-ers, that this plan was not thought to be a good one, and a new one was tried, and the whole fleet rode at anch-or through fierce gales, that test-ed the val-or of the men, more than any sea-fight they might take part in.

As the war went on, both North and South learned a great deal that they would not have thought of in times of peace, and had a chance to try men's souls as they had nev-er been tried be-fore, and to find out the stuff of which he-roes are made. For it is a well-known fact, that when the time of need comes, the right kind of men find their way to the front, and do deeds that not on-ly make their own names fa-mous, but prompt all boys to be brave and true, to stand man-ful-ly at the post where du-ty calls, and to die, if need be, for the cause they have at heart.

BLOCK-A-DING FLEET AT ANCH-OR.

CHAPTER IV.

THE BAT-TLE OF PORT ROY-AL.

By the first of June, 1861, the block-a-ding fleet made a line of float-ing bat-ter-ies all a-long the east-ern coast of the U-ni-ted States. Those in the South At-lan-tic squad-ron, soon found there was need of a coal-yard in some South-ern port, as it was a hard task to take on coal when the high winds blew, and the seas were rough. If they did not do this in time, they must go for coal a-round Cape Hat-te-ras, and up in-to Hamp-ton-Roads, in the State of Vir-gin-ia. This was a long and a hard trip of 100 miles or more, and if ves-sels should chance to be caught in the storms, that are no-where so fierce as they are off Cape Hat-ter-as, it would be hard to tell when they would get back, if they got back at all. Then, too, their ab-sence for coal made a bad break in the block-ade, and it was thought best to seize some port in the South, that it would take less time to reach, and stock it with coal for the use of the At-lan-tic squad-rons.

The WA-BASH with-drew from the fleet, and set out

for New York to fit her-self out as a flag-ship, and to take the lead in this new move-ment. Her flag of-fi-cer was Sam-u-el Fran-cis Du-pont, and her com-mand-er C. R. P. Rod-gers.

Ves-sels, fer-ry boats, and freight steam-ers of small size were bought and sent to Hamp-ton Roads, where there was a great crowd of boats wait-ing for or-ders. Those that were to be in com-mand of Flag Of-fi-cer Du-pont were filled with stores and coal, and on the 18th of Oc-to-ber, the Wa-bash came with four gun-boats. Steam trans-ports that had on board a force of 12,000 men, were al-so fit-ted out with food and ar-my stores of all kinds; and a light-draft steam-er, called the GOV-ERN-OR, with 600 sea-men on board, in com-mand of Ma-jor John G. Rey-nolds, was ad-ded to the fleet.

This queer lot of boats, to the num-ber of 50, or more, with the flag-ship at the head, steamed out of Hamp-ton Roads on the morn-ing of the 20th of Oc-to-ber. They went un-der sealed or-ders, not know-ing where they were to land, and moved at a slow rate of speed to-ward Cape Hat-ter-as, which it took them ten days to reach. The wind was strong from the east, and the sea rough, and the force of the cur-rent made two of the trans-ports strike on the shoals, and at once the fleet took a more east-er-ly course, and came up near the coast a-gain af-ter they had passed Cape Hat-ter-as.

On the first of No-vem-ber the wind blew a gale, and grave fears were felt, as most of the ves-sels were not fit for rough seas, and some of them were so load-ed that it seemed as if they must go down.

The night grew dark; the sea was a great sheet of foam; the an-gry waves beat high, and the rain struck

THE STORM AT PORT ROY-AL.

the fa-ces of the men with such force, as to make them feel as if they were be-ing pel-ted with small stones.

When day-light came, but one gun-boat was in sight from the mast-head of the flag-ship; but as the day wore on oth-er ves-sels came up and fol-lowed in her wake.

On the 3rd, the flag-ship drew near the SEN-E-CA and sent word for her com-mand-er to come on board. Or-ders were giv-en him, and he set out at once for Charles-ton Bar, which was 30 miles off. As soon as the SEN-E-CA came in sight of the forts, a sig-nal gun was fired. In a short time an-oth-er was heard from a point fur-ther in. These were to warn the folks in Charles-ton, that a ship of war had just come in sight, and was on its way to-ward the har-bor.

In some way the head reb-els had found out to what port the flag-ship was bound, and word was sent down the coast, for those on guard there to be on the watch for them. This was strange, as those who got up the scheme had made up their minds, but a few days be-fore, that an at-tack should be made on Port Roy-al, and it was thought that no one else knew a word a-bout it. But "walls have ears," spies are thick in war-times, and it is hard to tell friends from foes. Some of the smart-est nav-al of-fi-cers had gone with the South, and they, of course, knew well that there was no har-bor on the South-ern coast, as fine as that of Port Roy-al—in South Car-o-li-na.

Hil-ton Head was on the east, and Bay Point on the west, and ten miles in be-tween the san-dy shores lay the bar of Port Roy-al. Ves-sels of light draft, and some of the gun-boats were sent in to feel their way, and to make a chan-nel for the lar-ger ves-sels. This was done with great speed, so that in a short time a num-ber of the ves-sels were well placed, and safe from the strong sea-gales, and at the first high tide the whole fleet rode in o-ver the bar.

The three gun-boats, the OT-TA-WA, SEN-E-CA, PEM-BI-NA, and PEN-GUIN, had dropped their anch-ors out-side of the head-lands, on which the earth-works of the reb-els could be seen with-out the aid of a glass. Near sun-set three steam-ers came out from the head-lands, and at long-range fired on these boats, which at once got un-der way and sped to-ward the foe, and sent such a fire of shot from their guns, that the three steam-ers, in charge of Com-mo-dore Tat-nall, were forced to re-treat.

Soon af-ter sun-rise the next day—the 5th of No-vem-ber—the same trick was tried, just at the time that Flag

Of-fi-cer Rodg-ers had gone on board the OT-TA-WA, to take a look at the earth-works of the foe. The OT-TA-WA made signs to the SEN-E-CA, the CUR-LEW, and the I-SAAC SMITH, to draw near, and all stood in and sent such a storm of fire from their guns, that they drove Tat-nall's steam-ers back to the head-lands, and brought on them-selves a cross-fire from Fort Walk-er on Hil-ton Head, and Fort Beau-re-gard on Bay Point.

The rig-ging of the gun-boats was some-what torn by the shells from the earth-works, but a-side from that there was no harm done. The next day the wind blew so strong that the flag-of-fi-cer did not think it best to be-gin the at-tack, but on the 7th the sky was clear, the sea calm, and at day-light the flag-ship gave the sig-nals for the fleet to weigh anch-or, and to "form line of bat-tle."

This is the way in which they stood: The flag-ship WA-BASH, Com-mand-er C. R. P. Rodg-ers lead-ing; side-wheel steam frig-ate SUS-QUE-HAN-NA, Cap-tain Lard-ner; Sloop MO-HI-CAN, Com-mand-er Go-don; Sloop SEM-I-NOLE, Com-mand-er Gil-lis; Sloop PAW-NEE, Lieu-ten-ant-Com-mand-ing R. H. Wy-man; gun-boat U-NA-DIL-LA, Lieu-ten-ant-Com-mand-ing Na-po-le-on Col-lins; gun-boat OT-TA-WA, Lieu-ten-ant-Com-mand-ing Thomas H. Ste-vens; gun-boat PEM-BI-NA, Lieu-ten-ant-Com-mand-ing John P. Bank-head, and sail-sloop VAN-DA-LI-A, Com-mand-er Fran-cis S. Hag-ger-ty, towed by the I-SAAC SMITH, in com-mand of Lieu-ten-ant Nich-ol-son.

On the flank of these were the BI-EN-VILLE, Com-mand-er Charles Steed-man, lead-ing; the gun-boat SEN-E-CA, com-mand-ed by Lieu-ten-ant Am-men; gun-boat PEN-GUIN, in com-mand of Lieu-ten-ant P. A. Budd, and the AU-GUS-TA, Com-mand-er E. G. Par-rott.

The main col-umn as it went in was to fire on Fort Walk-er, and the flank-ing col-umn to fire on Fort Beau-re-gard; and when they were at a point, where their guns could not be turned on the reb-el earth-works, the ves-sels were to head round, and pass out to sea in the same way that they had come in. This game of "fol-low my lead-er" was to be kept up un-til the forts were ta-ken, or un-til fur-ther or-ders from the of-fi-cer of the flag-ship.

Tat-nall's ves-sels lay in range of the earth-works, but they were built of too light wood to make them of much use as men-of-war, and the guns they bore, though of new style, were not of the best kind, and were no match for those on board our boats.

The guns on the at-tack-ing fleet were poised with

11.—BOMBARDMENT OF PORT ROYAL.

great care, so that the shells fell fast in-side the earth-works, where they burst with great force, threw sand in-to the guns, and made such a stir, that the gun-ners could not take aim, or re-turn fire as fast as they want-ed to.

The troops in the fort had felt sure that their guns would soon sink and de-stroy the fleet, but when they saw the ves-sels come up, and pour forth a broad-side of shells, and then turn and send a rain of fire right in-to the earth-works, that did them much harm, they lost heart, for they were not used to this kind of war-fare. For four hours and a half they had stood at their posts, but when they saw the guns bro-ken, and the guns' crews kill-ed or wound-ed, they made up their minds to re-treat.

The flag-ship came round for the third time, and brought her guns to bear on Fort Walk-er. The shot cut through the air, the smoke died down, and there was no re-ply from the reb-el earth-works. The bat-tle of Port Roy-al was at an end! The foe had fled! and by half-past two in the af-ter-noon, the flag of the U-ni-on waved o-ver Fort Walk-er.

The cheers from the fleet were heard at Fort Beau-re-gard, and all there knew what they meant, and felt that their force was too small to hold out a-gainst such odds. So the men were told to spike their guns, spoil all the pow-der, and take up the line of march to Ed-ding's Isl-and. The troops on Bay Point al-so stole away, and did not take time to fold their tents.

The reb-els made their es-cape from Hil-ton Head by means of steam-boats that came up through Scull Creek, where there was a wharf a-bout six miles from the fort.

HOIST-ING THE FLAG.

At day-light on the 8th, the com-mand-ing of-fi-cer of the SEN-E-CA land-ed at Bay Point, and with thir-ty armed men went on shore, and hoist-ed the flag of the U-ni-on, on the flag-staff o-ver a small frame house, which the foe had made their head-quar-ters. Not a thing could be found; but in the camp, half a mile off, there were signs that the flight had been made in great

FLIGHT OF THE GAR-RI-SON.

haste. The tents were left stand-ing, with clothes, small arms, and a host of things in them, that the troops would on no ac-count, have gone with-out, if they had had time to stop and pick them up. A sol-dier was found in one of the tents, who had a bad wound, and could not leave with the rest of his com-rades, and this and a flock of tur-keys were all the signs of life on Bay Point.

At Hil-ton Head great guns were found in first-rate or-der; large chests full of pow-der; plen-ty of shot and shell, and tools of all sorts.

TROOPS DIS-EM-BARK-ING.

On the af-ter-noon of the 8th, Gen-er-al Thomas W. Sher-man came on board the SEN-E-CA, and went in her some miles up the Beau-fort Riv-er to see how the land lay. Not a fort was in sight; not a sign of earth-works on creek or riv-er; and so most of the troops from the trans-ports were put on shore at Hil-ton Head, where they be-gan at once to build a large camp.

The U-na-dil-la was sent up Broad Riv-er, and the Sen-e-ca, Pem-bi-na and Pen-guin went to Beau-fort, for it was thought that reb-el guns might be found on shore, and if so, these boats were to get out of the range of them, and send word to the flag-of-fi-cer, so that a force might be sent to their aid.

As the boats drew near a strip of low-land, not far from Beau-fort, the men on board saw a great crowd run-ning here and there, some on foot and some on horse-back. Crowds of ne-groes were in the streets. Thieves went in-to hou-ses and stole all they could lay their hands on, and seized all the boats and scows they could find in which to stow the goods.

The black folks were wild with joy. Their mas-ters had run off and left them free to do as they liked, and with more wealth than they knew what to do with. But one white man was found, and he was in such a state, from too much rum or too much fright, that it was of no use to try to talk with him, and so he was left on shore, and told that no harm would be done to him so long as he kept the peace.

When the ves-sels got back to Port Roy-al, boat-crews of ne-groes came on board, who said that a lot of slaves had been shot by their mas-ters whom they had not cho-sen to fol-low. The ne-groes were told that they would be ta-ken care of if they would serve the old flag, so they said they would first go to Beau-fort and then to Hil-ton Head, and bring with them all the black folks, who were in great fear that their mas-ters would kill them.

South Car-o-li-na was the first State to break loose from the U-ni-on, and those who dwelt there—black and white—were taught to shun all those who came from the North, and to do them all the harm that they could. There is no-thing that takes such deep root and grows so fast as ill-will, and it was a bold move to send a fleet down to this proud state, and to turn a part of this "sa-cred soil" in-to a coal yard! It was like "beard-ing the li-on in his den!"

Gen-er-al Dray-ton, who had charge of Fort Walk-er and Fort Beau-re-gard, had in his flight left a chart of the coast, with red marks on it, here and there, to show where oth-er forts had been built, and this was of great use to Flag Of-fi-cer Du-pont.

The loss of Port Roy-al, with all the guns and the earth-works that had been built for its de-fence, was a great blow to the South; and to gain such a great prize at so small a cost—for but eight men were killed—was a source of great joy to the whole North, but most of all to the South At-lan-tic Squad-ron. It took some time to make the block-ade as strong as there was need it should be, for all a-round Port Roy-al were creeks, and riv-ers, and roads that must be shut off, and both ar-my and na-vy found much work to do on land and shore.

In the mean-time the reb-els were at work in the rear, and had made up a plan to swoop down on the reg-i-ments of blue-coats at Beau-fort, and at Port Roy-al. Some of the slaves had gone back to their mas-ters, and some were made use of as spies to let the reb-els know how large a force there was of North-ern troops, and just how they were placed.

As soon as this came to the ears of Gen-er-al Thom-as Sher-man, he at once sent a let-ter to Com-mand-er Rodg-ers, and told him to charge on the foe. So the flag-ship, gun-boats, and tugs with great guns on board, set out in line of bat-tle, part of them go-ing up Beau-fort Riv-er, and part of them up Broad Riv-er. The at-tack was to be made on the first of Jan-u-a-ry, 1862, and at day-light the troops were un-der way, and made their first land-ing on a small isle, on the north bank of the Coo-saw. At this point the gun-boats came up and dropped anch-or, and soon shells were thrown in-to the earth-works of the reb-els, at Port Roy-al Fer-ry.

No fire came from the fort, and so the troops went on, and the boats pushed their way through the nar-row chan-nels, send-ing shot and shell in-to the woods, and dri-ving the reb-els from their camps and earth-works.

The next day the reb-els were well out of range, and the whole of Port Roy-al was in the hands of the U-ni-on men, and the South did not try a-gain to wrest it from them.

Flag Of-fi-cer Du-pont, and Com-mand-er Rodg-ers won much praise for what they had done, and were soon sent off to cruise on the coasts of Geor-gi-a and Flor-i-da, and were next heard of at Ty-bee sound.

This seems to be the place to tell the sto-ry of Rob-ert Small, a slave, and the pi-lot of the PLAN-TER, which ves-sel was made use of to car-ry guns and stores to the reb-el ar-my. On the morn-ing of May 13, the PLAN-TER lay at the Charles-ton wharf close to the ar-my head-quar-ters, with steam up and the cap-tain on shore. Small cast off the ropes, and passed the forts with the reb-el flag fly-ing, gave the u-su-al sa-lute, and when out of range of their guns sent up a white flag, just in time to save him from be-ing fired at, by one of the block-a-ding ves-sels. The PLAN-TER was armed with a 32-pound piv-ot gun, a 24-pound how-itz-er, and had on board four great guns, that were to have been placed in a new fort, on the mid-dle ground in Charles-ton Har-bor. Eight men, five wo-men, and three chil-dren were on board of the ves-sel. Small was the bright-est and smart-est ne-gro that had come in-to the U-ni-on lines, and was of great use as a pi-lot on the South-ern coast. He served in this way, till the end of the war, and then was sent to Wash-ing-ton as a mem-ber of Con-gress, from the State of South Car-o-li-na

ES-CAPE OF THE PLAN-TER.

CHAPTER V.

THE MON-I-TOR AND THE MER-RI-MAC.

WHILE the South was at work on the MER-RI-MAC, in the Nor-folk na-vy yard, the North was hard at work in the Brook-lyn na-vy yard, ma-king an i-ron clad that it was thought would beat her.

A man, named John E-rics-son, had drawn the plans of a ves-sel which was like a steam bat-ter-y, and sent them to the Sec-re-ta-ry of the Na-vy, Gid-e-on Welles. Welles, and those with whom he sought coun-sel, liked the plans, and word was sent to have the work be-gun at once. The keel was laid in the yard at Green-point, in the month of Oc-to-ber, 1861, and in three months the new i-ron clad was read-y to be launched.

The name MON-I-TOR, was giv-en to her by E-rics-son him-self, and it has since been the name of all war ves-sels of that class.

The new boat had a small i-ron hull on which was a large raft. In the cen-ter of this raft was a tur-ret, that could be moved round by means of a crank, in which were two 11-inch smooth bores, that sent sol-id shot weigh-ing 180 pounds. In front of the tur-ret was the pi-lot house, built like an i-ron log-hut with "peep holes," through which those in-side could look out and see what was go-ing on. The roof of the pi-lot house was a great i-ron plate an inch and a half thick, rest-ing on the walls by its own weight. In a fight the smoke-stacks were to be ta-ken a-part and laid on the deck, the draught for the en-gines be-ing kept up by a great blow-ing ma-chine.

None but brave men would trust them-selves at sea in such a queer craft as this, and Lieut. John L. Wor-den was put in com-mand of her while she was still on the stocks.

He was to pick out his crews from the re-ceiv-ing ships NORTH CAR-O-LI-NA and the SA-BINE, "and a bet-ter one," said Wor-den, "no na-val com-mand-er ev-er had the hon-or to com-mand." They were all young men, and when told the style of ves-sel they were to go in, the foe they would have to meet, and the hard-ships they would have to en-dure, they did not shrink or turn back, but were brave and bold from first to last.

Wor-den chose Lieu-ten-ant S. Da-na Green, a boy of 22 years, to be his chief of-fi-cer, and the choice proved to be a wise one.

On Thurs-day morn-ing, March 6, 1862, the MON-I-TOR left New York in tow of the tug boat, SETH Low, and by af-ter-noon was well out to sea. The next day a strong breeze from the north-west made the sea so rough that the waves broke o-ver the ves-sel's deck, and poured in floods un-der the tur-ret. The smoke-pipe and blow-er-pipe were quite low, and by af-ter-noon the sea rose so that it swept o-ver them, and the rush of wa-ter stopped the draught in the fur-nace, and filled the

THE MON-I-TOR AT SEA.

en-gine-room and fire-room with gas. The en-gi-neers and fire-men tried their best to mend the breaks that had been made, but the gas choked up their lungs so that they could not breathe, and they were drawn out of the en-gine room just in time to save their lives.

The hand-pump was used, and the men set to bail-ing,

but no good was done as the sea came in fast-er than it could be put out. The tug head-ed for shore, and at the end of five hours brought the MON-I-TOR in-to smooth wa-ter, the en-gine room was cleared of gas, the bro-ken bands mend-ed, and the i-ron-clad set out a-gain to-ward Hamp-ton Roads. All went well un-til mid-night, when the MON-I-TOR crossed a shoal, and ran in-to a strong head-sea. The waves swept the deck and made their way through the pipes, and in-to the en-gine room, and the men were in great dan-ger. The head-winds made the boat pitch and toss most wild-ly, but the tow-ropes held, and at the end of five long hours day-light broke; the tug had or-ders to move near shore, the MON-I-TOR was once more in smooth wa-ters, and on the 8th of March, at four o'-clock in the af-ter-noon, she passed Cape Hen-ry.

The day af-ter the MON-I-TOR left New York, the big i-ron-clad MER-RI-MAC steamed out of Nor-folk, and up the E-liz-a-beth Riv-er to Hamp-ton Roads. The war ships CON-GRESS and CUM-BER-LAND, both made of wood, lay off New-port News, where they had been for some months as part of the James Riv-er block-ade. Sev-en miles off, at Fort-ress Mon-roe, were the war frig-ates MIN-NE-SO-TA, RO-AN-OKE and ST. LAW-RENCE.

THE MER-RI-MAC AP-PEARS.

The Con-gress was off on a long cruise when the war broke out, and when she came back in Jan-u-a-ry, her crew, who had served their full time were sent to the North, and new men taken in their stead. So few were these in num-ber that the 99th New York—or "U-ni-on Coast Guard"—had or-ders to go on board, but e-ven then the ill-fa-ted ves-sel was poor-ly manned.

The Cum-ber-land, how-ev-er, had a first-class crew un-der the com-mand of Cap-tain Rad-ford, who had gone to at-tend a court of in-qui-ry on board the frig-ate Ro-an-oke. His place was filled by Lieu-ten-ant George Mor-ris. Lieu-ten-ant Jo-seph Smith com-mand-ed the Con-gress.

The flag of-fi-cer of the MER-RI-MAC was Com-mo-dore Frank-lin Bu-chan-an, and he had un-der his com-mand a fine lot of of-fi-cers, and a crew of 300 brave men. They were all stran-gers to each oth-er and to the ship, and there had been no chance to put them through a-ny sort of drill, to teach them how to use the guns, and how to man-age such a float-ing mon-ster.

It was known at the North that the reb-els had raised the MER-RI-MAC, and were fit-ting her up for a great fight, but it was not known that she would be shot-proof un-der the fire of such broad-sides as the CON-GRESS and the CUM-BER-LAND could send a-gainst her.

There had been a light rain on the 7th of March, which had wet the sails of the CON-GRESS and the CUM-BER-LAND, and they were loosed to dry in the bright sun that shone on the morn-ing of the 8th. Washed clothes hung in the rig-ging, and the sail-ors lounged a-round wish-ing they had some-thing to do, for they were tired of ri-ding at anch-or, when the MER-RI-MAC hove in sight, look-ing, as the pi-lot of the CUM-BER-LAND said, like "a huge croc-o-dile," and made its way right to-ward them.

The CUM-BER-LAND was at once put in fight-ing trim, and wheeled round so as to place her broad-side to-ward the MER-RI-MAC, and the young com-mand-er of the CON-

GRESS gave or-ders to "beat to quar-ters," and put things in ship-shape to meet the ad-van-cing foe.

"From the camp on shore, at New-port News," writes one of the he-roes, "came the sound of the 'long roll' that roused the troops to arms, and each man felt that some great deed was to be done that day, but did not dream that the great-est nav-al bat-tle of the age would be fought be-fore the sun went down."

A lit-tle af-ter two o'clock in the af-ter-noon the MER-RI-MAC came with-in range and o-pened fire from her bow gun. The CON-GRESS sent back a fire of shot, that rat-tled down the sides of the mon-ster like peb-bles from a slant-ing roof, and the MER-RI-MAC kept on its way to-ward the CUM-BER-LAND, which gave her a sa-lute of shot that swept off a few of her men, and did some harm to her guns, but did not stop her course.

With bows on, the MER-RI-MAC struck the CUM-BER-LAND with such force, that she drove the i-ron ram so far in-to the planks that it was bro-ken off, and made such a hole in the side of the sloop-of-war that a full stream of wa-ter rush-ed in. At the same time the black mon-ster sent a fierce broad-side at point-blank range, that mowed down of-fi-cers, gun-ners, sail-ors and all be-fore it.

The bow of the CUM-BER-LAND soon be-gan to sink,

THE FIGHT WITH THE CUM-BER-LAND.

and her fate was sure. "Sur-ren-der that ship, Mor-ris, or I'll sink her!" cried Lieu-ten-ant Jones, who had been a school-mate of Lieu-ten-ant Mor-ris, out of one of the port-holes of the MER-RI-MAC.

"Ne-ver!" cried Mor-ris. "I'll go down with her first!"

The red flag, mean-ing "no sur-ren-der," was run up to the CUM-BER-LAND's fore-truck; the gun's crews kicked off their shoes and stripped to the waist; tanks of car-tridges were brought on the gun-deck, and round af-ter round was fired at the i-ron clad.

The decks were strewn with the dead and dy-ing, and were slip-per-y with blood. One poor fel-low was pin-

ON THE DECK OF THE CUM-BER-LAND.

ned down with a great splin-ter of wood through his chest. The cap-tain of one of the guns had both legs shot off be-low the knee, yet he made out to crawl to his gun and pull the string, and then fell back dead. An old man-of-war's man was ta-ken be-low, with both legs off, and still made out to cheer, and say, "Boys, stand by your guns!"

As the wa-ters rose the wound-ed were lif-ted up on racks and mess-chests to keep them from be-ing drowned; and the guns were fired af-ter the wa-ter was knee-deep on the CUM-BER-LAND. Then Lieu-ten-ant Mor-ris cried out, "Up, my brave boys, and save your-selves! Ev-er-y man for him-self, and God for us all!"

the last gun was fired, the ship keeled o-ver, and of-fi-cers and crew jumped for their lives in-to the wa-ter. All of the boats had been shot a-way but one, and this was soon filled. Some of the men were shot by the guns of the i-ron clad, as soon as they rose to the sur-face of the wa-ter, and a few who could swim made their way to-ward New-port News, which they reached in safe-ty. Mor-ris was saved by his men, and the CUM-BER-LAND went down in 54 feet of wa-ter with the red flag—" *No sur-ren-der*"—still float-ing from her top-mast.

THE FLAG STILL WAVES.

While the fight went on be-tween the MER-RI-MAC and CUM-BER-LAND, three steam-ers, the PAT-RICK HEN-RY, JAMES-TOWN, and TEX-AS which lay at the mouth of the James Riv-er, o-pened fire on the CON-GRESS, and did her much harm. Smith, see-ing the fate of the CUM-BER-LAND, made up his mind to run a-shore, and so get out of the way of the reb-el ram, and wait un-til the rest of the frig-ates came up. But as soon as the CON-GRESS was hard and fast on the flats, the MER-RI-MAC came up on her stern and at a dis-tance of

150 yards raked her fore and aft with shot and shell. The three small steam-ers joined in, and as the CON-GRESS could only re-ply with her two stern guns, the reb-els had things all their own way.

The fight was kept up for an hour. The old frig-ate was but a tar-get for the reb-el guns. No ves-sels came to her aid. Her decks were strewn with the dead and the dy-ing. Her com-mand-er was killed; and Lieu-ten-ant Pen-der-grast, who took his place, find-ing that naught was to be gained by the shed-ding of more blood, ran up the white flag, and gave his sword and col-ors to Lieu-ten-ant Par-ker of the Beau-fort, who told him to go back to his ship and have the wound-ed ta-ken off at once.

Mean-while the Fed-er-al force at Fort But-ler, in com-mand of Gen-er-al Mans-field, kept up a fire on the reb-el gun-boats; the shore was lined with troops, and the sharp-shoot-ers from their ri-fle pits picked off of-fi-cers and men from the decks, and from the rig-ging.

Reb-el of-fi-cers cried out to Gen-er-al Mans-field to cease fi-ring, and point-ed to the white flag on the CON-GRESS. "The ship may float the white flag," shout-ed the Gen-er-al, "but we don't."

Bu-chan-an, find-ing that he could not take the CON-

SUR-REN-DER OF THE CON-GRESS.

GRESS, gave or-ders that she should be fired with hot shot, and in a short time she was in flames fore and aft. Night came on, and the MER-RI-MAC with-drew to Sew-all's Point, well pleased with her af-ter-noon's work, and her mind made up to at-tack the MIN-NE-SO-TA the next day.

No one on board the CON-GRESS knew just when she would blow up, so the men had to work hard and fast in the sti-fling smoke, to get the wound-ed on deck and in-to the boats that were to take them to shore. It was dark when the last trip was made, and the ship was left to its fate with the dead ly-ing just as they fell. It was a strange, weird sight to see the ship on fire, and the flames dyed the waters red, and lit up the white tents on both sides of the stream.

At mid-night the CON-GRESS blew up with a noise that was heard for miles and miles, and then all was still.

BLOW-ING UP OF THE CON-GRESS.

On the af-ter-noon of the 8th, the MON-I-TOR passed Cape Hen-ry, and in the e-ven-ing steamed in-to Hampton Roads, drew near the MIN-NE-SO-TA, which was a-ground, and then learned the fate of the two war ships. The men on the MIN-NE-SO-TA, as soon as they saw the i-ron clad, knew that she must be the one that had been build-ing at Green-point, and could not but smile at her size, and think what a poor chance she would have in a fight with the reb-el ram.

Sun-day, the 9th of March, 1862, was a calm, clear day, and at half-past sev-en in the morn-ing the MER-RI-MAC left Sew-all's Point, steered to-ward the MIN-NE-SO-TA, and o-pened fire on her while yet a mile a-way. Bu-chan-an was laid up with a wound, and the ram was in charge of Lieu-ten-ant Jones. Though the men on board of the MON-I-TOR had been in dan-ger of two ship-wrecks, and had not had much chance to eat or to sleep, they did not stop to think of these things, but at once cleared the decks, drew up her anch-or, and made haste to meet the mon-ster foe.

As the low black ob-ject came out from be-hind the MIN-NE-SO-TA, the eyes of all on ship and on shore were on the strange craft. Where had she been? Where did she come from? Some said she looked like "a cheese-box on a raft." Some said she was like "a tin can on a shin-gle." All made fun of her, and were sur-prised that so small a boy should be sent to do a man's work.

The MON-I-TOR drew out in-to the stream a-way from the frig-ate and steered for the star-board bow of the MER-RI-MAC, then changed its course and fired on the reb-el ram. Shell and shot, and mus-ket balls were sent back, and flew o-ver the low deck, but did no harm.

Act-ing Mas-ter Stod-der was lean-ing a-gainst the

tur-ret when a shot struck the out-er wall and stun-ned him so that he had to be put on the sick list. Once in a while the tur-ret would catch,—for the ves-sel had been built in such haste that all her parts did not work just right—but it would ere long be set free, and go round and round, the same as ev-er, deal-ing out hot shot.

Wor-den passed at the stern of the MER-RI-MAC and tried to break up her screw, but missed it by a few feet. Then he went by on the port side, still keep-ing up a stead-y fire. At times the two boats were so close that they touched each oth-er, but no dam-age seemed to be done to ei-ther, and at last the MER-RI-MAC turned and made an at-tack on the MIN-NE-SO-TA. The frig-ate gave her a broad-side of guns, that would have blown her to bits had she been made of wood, but the shot struck harm-less on her i-ron roof, and dropped in-to the wa-ters be-yond.

The MER-RI-MAC re-plied with a shell from her bow-gun that went through the berth-deck a-mid-ships, tore four rooms in-to one, and set the ves-sel on fire. The flames were soon put out. A sec-ond shell set one of the tug-boats on fire.

Fif-ty sol-id shot from the MIN-NE-SO-TA rat-tled a-gainst the MER-RI-MAC like so ma-ny hail-stones. A third shell was sent from the reb-el ram, which then drew off and set out to drive at a full head of speed, and serve the MIN-NE-SO-TA as she had done the CUM-BER-LAND.

Wor-den saw the move-ment, put his helm hard-a-port, and re-ceived the blow on his star-board side, where it glanced off and did no harm. Wor-den's post on board the MON-I-TOR had been in the pi-lot house, from the "peep holes" of which he could see all that took place. Greene was in charge of the tur-ret and the bat-ter-y. Act-ing Mas-ter Stod-der was first at the wheel, and when he was hurt Chief En-gi-neer Stimes took his place, and did the best that he could to keep the tur-ret mo-ving. Act-ing Mas-ter Web-ber had charge of the pow-der on the berth-deck, and the pay-mas-ter and Cap-tain's clerk, both on the berth deck, passed the or-ders from the pi-lot house.

Shut in in this way, it was hard for the men to tell where they were, or just what was go-ing on out-side, but still they fought on with brave true hearts. Though stran-gers to Wor-den when he took com-mand, they soon be-came fond of him, and made up their minds to stand by him so long as he had need of their help. And soon the whole weight of the fight was laid on the shoul-ders of these young he-roes.

The MER-RI-MAC, which had tried its best to sink and to blow up the MON-I-TOR, now aimed its guns at the pi-lot house on the deck of the raft. This was the weakest part of the MON-I-TOR, and at noon a shell struck the wall, the roof was lif-ted half way off and Wor-den's eyes were filled with pow-der and bits of i-ron. Blind as he was, he could see the light from the roof, and gave or-ders at once to have the boat sheer off; but as tel-e-phones were un-known in those days, and all on board were more or less dazed by the shock, it took some time for the or-der to be car-ried out, and for word to reach the tur-ret of what had ta-ken place in the pi-lot house.

CAP-TAIN WOR-DEN IN THE PI-LOT HOUSE.

When Lieu-ten-ant Greene went for-ward he found the cap-tain at the foot of the lad-der stunned and help-less, with his face black and stream-ing with blood. He was at once put in the sur-geon's care, and Greene went in-to the pi-lot house, and Stimes took his place in the tur-ret. Du-ring this time, when there was no cap-tain at the helm, the MON-I-TOR steamed a-way with no one to guide her, and it was thought that she had with-drawn from the fight. Those on board the Min-ne-so-ta felt that all hope was lost, and the cap-tain was a-bout to set the ship on fire, so that it should not fall in-to the hands of the reb-els, when the pluck-y lit-tle Mon-i-tor once more faced the might-y Mer-ri-mac.

To her great sur-prise she saw the reb-el ram was on its way to Sew-all's Point. The field was clear! There was no foe to fight! A few shots were fired af-ter her, but the Mer-ri-mac did not re-turn them, and when Wor-den was told what had ta-ken place, joy filled his heart, and he ex-claimed, as did Gen-er-al Wolfe at the bat-tle of Que-bec, "Then I can die hap-py!" But he did not die un-til long years af-ter this, and in 1863 we read of his be-ing in com-mand of the Mon-i-tor Mon-tauk, a bet-ter and sa-fer boat to be in than the one, that in spite of her weak-ness, had put to flight the mon-ster Mer-ri-mac.

What a vic-to-ry for the U-ni-on flag! What a tri-umph for the North! and for John E-rics-son! and what a proud day for Lieu-ten-ant Greene, the young he-ro of the bold Mon-i-tor!

Hamp-ton Roads was free! The fleet were saved! and as if the fame of these two ves-sels was to rest on this one great deed, it was the first and last fight of the

Mon-i-tor, and the Mer-ri-mac. The lat-ter was ta-ken to Nor-folk, and placed in dry dock to have a new ram put in, to take the place of the one that was broken off in the Cum-ber-land, and one morn-ing in A-pril steamed down in-to Hamp-ton Roads, with Com-mo-dore Tat-nall in com-mand.

He had not been there long be-fore he heard that the U-ni-ted States troops were on their way to Nor-folk, and he be-gan at once to strip the ship, and then set it on fire so that it should not fall in-to U-ni-on hands. The of-fi-cers and men made their es-cape by

BLOW-ING UP OF THE MER-RI-MAC.

III.—BURN-ING OF THE NOR-FOLK NA-VY YARD.

way of Suf-folk, and on the 11th of May, 1862, the MER-RI-MAC blew up.

On the 29th of De-cem-ber, of that year, the MON-I-TOR set out for Beau-fort, North Car-o-li-na, in tow of the RHODE ISL-AND, and was wrecked in a storm off Cape Hat-ter-as. Ropes were thrown to the crew who clung round the tur-ret, but they failed to grasp them, and so went down with the ship as she sank in the rough wa-ters of the At-lan-tic.

WRECK OF THE MON-I-TOR.

CHAPTER VI.

DA-VID G. FAR-RA-GUT.

DA-VID GLAS-GOW FAR-RA-GUT, the first Ad-mi-ral of the U-ni-ted States, was born near Knox-ville, TEN-NES-SEE, on the 5th of Ju-ly, 1801. His fa-ther was a Ma-jor of Cav-al-ry.

In those days the In-di-ans did all they could to an-noy the white set-tlers, and one day a par-ty of the red men came to the house, while the fa-ther of young Da-vid was a-way from home. The moth-er, who was a strong, brave wo-man, barred the door, sent all the lit-tle ones in-to the loft of the barn, and stood on guard with an axe in her hand. The red men tried to get speech with her, but she kept them at bay, and at last they went off, no one could tell why, and were not seen a-gain in that part of the land.

In a few years Ma-jor Far-ra-gut was made a sail-ing mas-ter in the Na-vy, and placed in com-mand of a gun-boat at New Or-le-ans, and made his home at that place. In 1808 his wife died of yel-low fe-ver, leav-ing three boys and two girls, one of whom was a small babe.

In 1809 Sail-ing Mas-ter Far-ra-gut bought a farm of

900 a-cres on Pas-ca-gou-la Riv-er, and Da-vid went with the young man who was sent to clear the place. This was the first time the boy had been on salt wa-ter, and he "hoped, at that time, it would be his last." His fa-ther took the two in a small boat a-cross Lake Pont-char-train when the wind blew a gale, and felt not the least fear, for he thought his pi-rogue—a kind of ca-noe made of two pie-ces of wood in-stead of one—was far more safe than the gun-boats. They were hailed as they passed the gun-boats and told to come on board till the blow was o-ver, but the Sail-ing Mas-ter on the yawl boat said he could ride it out bet-ter than they could. He was fond of the sea, but his health was not strong e-nough for him to en-dure a long cruise, so he would make trips a-cross the Lake, with his chil-dren, in the yawl; and this he kept up till the day of his death.

When the weath-er was bad, they slept on the beach of some one of the small isles, and dug holes for beds, and heaped the sand up o-ver them for bed-clothes.

When the fa-ther was ta-ken to task for let-ting his chil-dren lead such a rough life, he said it was the way to make them brave and strong. And it was this sort of school-ing that made Da-vid so fond and fear-less of the sea, o'er which he loved to roam.

In the year 1812, when En-gland made war a-gainst A-mer-i-ca, and sent ships-of-war o-ver to fight our ships, it chanced that the boy, Da-vid Far-ra-gut, was on board the Es-sex, which was in com-mand of Com-mo-dore Por-ter, when it fought in Lake E-rie with the En-glish sloop-of-war A-LERT. At this time En-gland owned 1,000 ships-of-war, while A-mer-i-ca had but 20.

FAR-RA-GUT AS A MID-SHIP-MAN.

Por-ter was a friend of Da-vid's fa-ther and had giv-en the boy a mid-ship-man's berth. In this, his first fight, he met with a se-vere wound, but was so brave, and bore him-self so like a man, that Por-ter made men-tion of him in his re-port, and but for his youth he would at once have been pro-mo-ted.

Af-ter the bat-tle of Lake Erie, the Es-SEX was sent on a cruise in the Pa-cif-ic O-ce-an, and seized quite a num-ber of pri-zes, a-mong which were two Brit-ish whaleships—the GEOR-GI-AN-A and the POL-I-CY—both well armed and manned.

Part of the crews of both ships were A-mer-i-cans who had been forced to serve un-der the Brit-ish flag, which was the cause of the war of 1812. When the small boat drew near, which had been sent out from the Es-SEX, in com-mand of Lieu-ten-ant Downes, and the wha-lers saw the stars and stripes at her bow, they gave three cheers and cried, "We are all A-mer-i-cans!"

The GEOR-GI-AN-A was at once fit-ted out as a crui-ser with Downes as cap-tain, and Far-ra-gut as first-of-fi-cer. Once, when out in the gig, Downes gave or-ders to his men to run the boat on a small beach on one of the Gal-a-pa-gos isles. As they drew near shore they saw a lot of seals make for the wa-ter. The cap-tain told the men to try and kill one, so they made choice of a fine one and beat him o-ver the head with oars and boat-hooks; but he still kept on to-ward the wa-ter. At last one of the men caught hold of his tail, and thought he had him sure, but the seal dragged the whole crew, who had come to the aid of their com-rade, in-to the wat-er.

The cap-tain fired at the seal when he freed him-self from the men, but he sank out of sight.

When the gig got back to the ship, the wha-lers taught the men how to catch seals, and the next time they went out they were armed with clubs and knives, and oars with broad blades, and in time be-came quite skil-ful in their use.

But the next time they went out for seals they fell in with a sea-lion, who a-rose as soon as the boat came on shore, shook his head, and made a start for the wa-ter. "Now, boys," cried the cap-tain, "you have a chance to show your A-mer-i-can skill. String your-selves a-long, and each man stand read-y to give him a blow on the nose. One blow will fix him." But that blow was nev-er giv-en.

HUNT-ING SEA LIONS.

Far-ra-gut, who did not like the looks of the strange an-i-mal—part beast and part fish—ran and took a seat in one of the boats. With a fierce roar, the sea-li-on made a dash for the wa-ter, and the men did not wait to be told to get out of his way. Far-ra-gut had a good laugh at the Cap-tain, who charged him with be-ing a-fraid to stand on the beach; while Far-ra-gut claimed that he nev-er un-der-took to do a thing with-out go-ing through with it.

In the year 1843 Far-ra-gut mar-ried Vir-gin-i-a Loy-all, whose fa-ther was well known and much thought of in Nor-folk, Vir-gin-i-a, and in 1844 he was made an of-fi-cer on board the ship of the line PENN-SYL-VA-NI-A, which was then at Ports-mouth, in that State.

When the strife be-gan with Mex-i-co, in 1845, Far-ra-gut had asked that he might be sent to the seat of war, where he thought he could be of great use. He had spent some years in the Gulf, knew all a-bout the coast, and the strength of its forts, and had ta-ken pains to note all that he saw in the year 1838, when the French took the cas-tle of San Juan (*wan*) de Ul-lo-a.

He had made his boast that he could take the cas-tle of San Juan, with the PENN-SYL-VA-NI-A, and two sloops of war like the SAR-A-TO-GA, and was much laughed at for his fol-ly.

But "all things come to those who wait," and in the year 1847, Far-ra-gut was put in com-mand of the sloop-of-war SAR-A-TOGA, with or-ders to sail at once for Ve-ra Cruz, and in two days he was on his way. His crew was made up of such men as he could get from the oth-er ships, but one of whom was a trained sea-man; but he had them drill each day in the use of the guns, and in fi-ring at a mark, so that they were in fair trim when they reached Ve-ra Cruz. But they were just too late. San-ta An-na had sur-ren-dered to Gen-er-al Scott, March, 1847, and the stars and stripes waved proud-ly o-ver the walls of the fort.

Far-ra-gut took the yel-low fe-ver while off the coast of Mex-i-co, and was so ill that for a time it was thought that he could not live. His mind was not at ease, for he felt that our Na-vy would have won a high place, had her ships made the at-tack as they should have done, and he looked back on this cruise with no feel-ing of pride.

He was so vexed that he gave up his com-mand, and brought his ves-sel to New York, which port he reached Feb-ru-ary 19, 1848, paid off his crew, and left the sloop-of-war SAR-A-TO-GA in the Brook-lyn Na-vy yard.

For some time the head men at Wash-ing-ton, had thought that there should be a Na-vy yard on the Pa-cif-ic coast, and three Na-val of-fi-cers had been sent out to choose a good place. Choice was made of Mare Isl-and, Cal-i-for-ni-a, and in 1854, Far-ra-gut was sent there to be-gin the work.

He set sail with his wife and fam-i-ly in the STAR OF
THE WEST, and for sev-en months lived on board an old
sloop-of-war, that was ta-ken up San Pab-lo Bay and
moored near the yard. Valle-jo (*val-yo*), a small town
near at hand, soon showed signs of new life, and be-gan
to spread it-self so that there was quite a brisk trade in
town lots. Far-ra-gut spent four years on the coast of
Cal-i-for-ni-a, where he rode much on horse-back in the
fine air, and at the end of that time was in much bet-ter
health than he had been for some years.

In 1858 he sailed for New York by way of the Isth-
mus of Pan-a-ma, and was placed in com-mand of the
BROOK-LYN, one of the new sloops-of-war. He made a
tri-al trip in this ves-sel to Beau-fort, South Car-o-li-na,
where he met with great kind-ness, and soon af-ter had
or-ders to go to the Gulf of Mex-i-co.

It was no small task to man-age such a big ves-sel as
the BROOK-LYN, and to steer her course a-round the coast
of Mex-i-co, but Far-ra-gut seemed to en-joy it all the
more for the dan-ger there was in it.

He said he took as much pleas-ure in run-ning in-to
Ve-ra Cruz in a gale of wind, as ev-er a boy did in a-ny
feat of skill.

The sloop-of-war SAR-A-TO-GA was at Ve-ra Cruz at

the same time as the BROOK-LYN, and the crews of both ships kept up a round of sports—feats of skill and tests of strength—that made them bet-ter sea-men and marks-men.

In 1860 the BROOK-LYN passed out of his com-mand, and Far-ra-gut was on wait-ing or-ders at Nor-folk, Vir-gin-i-a. Here we find him when the war broke out. He had seen the cloud in the sky, that fore-told a storm was near, but was laughed at by those to whom he spoke of his fears.

"God for-bid," said he, "that I should have to raise my hand a-gainst the South!"—yet when the time came, he felt it would be his du-ty to set a-side all claims of friend-ship and all ties of blood, and cast his lot with those who stood by the Flag of our U-ni-on.

He was a frank, out-spo-ken man, and took no pains to hide his views, and when some one told him that Nor-folk was no place for a man to live in who thought and felt as he did, Far-ra-gut calm-ly said, "Well, I can live some-where else."

He went straight home and told his wife that he meant to "stick to the flag," and asked her to say at once wheth-er she would go North with him or stay at Nor-folk. She was as prompt to act as he was, and told her hus-band that she would go with him. With a sad heart Far-ra-gut turned his back on the South, for he felt that there was to be a great war, in which much blood would be spilt, and the end of which no mor-tal man could guess.

He reached Bal-ti-more on the 18th of A-pril, and found a great stir at that place. The Mas-sa-chu-setts troops—the van-guard of New En-gland—had been at-tacked, and the rail-road be-tween Bal-ti-more and Phil-a-del-phi-a had been cut in two by the ru-in of the bridge a-cross the Sus-que-han-na. Far-ra-gut crossed in a ca-nal-boat, and reached New York a-mid the din of drums, the march of troops com-ing and go-ing, and oth-er war-like sounds, and in a few days took a cot-tage- at the vil-lage of Has-tings-on-the Hud-son, where he meant to wait un-til he had or-ders to serve on ship-board.

CHAPTER VII.

ON THE MIS-SIS-SIP-PI.

On the 9th of Jan-u-a-ry, 1862, the Sec-re-ta-ry of War wrote to Far-ra-gut that he had been cho-sen to com-mand the West Gulf Squad-ron, and was to hoist his flag on board the U-ni-ted States steam-sloop-of-war HART-FORD.

His or-ders were to take New Or-le-ans, and it was late in Feb-ru-a-ry that he set out for the mouth of the Mis-sis-sip-pi Riv-er.

In the mean-time let us take a look at what was go-ing on at the head of this great riv-er.

In the first part of Feb-ru-a-ry, 1862, the West-ern Flo-til-la, in com-mand of Ad-mi-ral Foote, bore Gen-er-al Grant and his troops up the Ten-nes-see Riv-er, to at-tack Fort Hen-ry. The roads were so bad that the land force could not march with much speed, so that the at-tack had to be made by the gun-boats a-lone. As soon as the fort was in the hands of our men, the Flo-til-la went back to Cai-ro, Il-li-nois, to get mor-tar-boats to aid in an at-tack on Fort Don-el-son, on the Cum-ber-land Riv-er.

Foote did not have time to get the mor-tar-boats, but went up the Cum-ber-land with his flo-til-la of gun-boats, and be-gan the at-tack on the 14th, with four i-ron clad boats, and two of wood.

The reb-els were forced from their strong-holds a-long the shore, af-ter a sharp fight, and then the gun-boats with-drew with a loss of 54 men by death or wounds.

GUN-BOATS AT-TACK FORT DON-EL-SON.

The rest of the work of ta-king Fort Don-el-son was left to the ar-my, and on the 16th of Feb-ru-a-ry the reb-els laid down their arms, and the news sent a thrill of joy through the whole North. With the fort were ta-ken 13,500 men, 3,000 hor-ses, 48 can-non such as are used on the field of bat-tle, 17 large guns, 20,000 mus-kets, and a large stock of ar-my stores.

Af-ter the fall of Fort Don-el-son, Foote's flo-til-la found much work to do on the Mis-sis-sip-pi Riv-er, on both sides of which the reb-els had built strong-holds, so that from end to end there was a long line of forts.

The Mis-sis-sip-pi Riv-er ri-ses in the high-lands of Min-ne-so-ta, and winds its way south-ward—like a great sea-ser-pent—for a dis-tance of 2,986 miles. It emp-ties it-self in-to the Gulf of Mex-i-co through five great mouths, called Pass-es.

On both sides of the riv-er are num-bers of small creeks and lakes, and bay-ous (*bi-oos*), and for some parts of the year the whole of this re-gion is un-der wa-ter, ow-ing to the o-ver-flow of the Mis-sis-sip-pi. Dense for-ests of cot-ton-wood, tu-lip trees, sweet gum, mag-no-li-a, syc-a-more, and ash, are found here, with deep jun-gles of cane and vine. Cy-press swamps al-so a-bound.

When Por-ter went with five i-ron clads and four mor-tar boats to aid Gen-er-al Grant, in his at-tack on Vicks-burg, he found it a hard task to force his way through the Ya-zoo pass.

The reb-els had a force of at least 4,000 men in the swamps, and forced the ne-groes at the muz-zle of the gun to fell trees all a-round the fleet, in the rear as well as in the front.

The gun-boats moved like snails, but with great pow-er, push-ing a-side all sap-lings, bush-es, and drift-wood that came in their way. The turns were so short, that the Ad-mi-ral had to heave his ves-sel round the bends with not a foot of space to spare. It took him, at this rate, 24 hours to go four miles, and this meant not on-ly slow work but hard work.

The *bay-ous* were nar-row and crook-ed, the turns sud-den, and the chan-nel was half filled with cy-press and wil-lows that grew in the bed of the stream. Now and then a thick-et of trees o-ver head had to be thrust a-side, and the i-ron clads broke the bran-ches of the for-est, knocked down trees, and tore up roots in a way that gave de-light to troops and tars whose hearts beat true un-der jack-ets of blue.

Trees had to be pulled up by the roots, and stumps sawed off be-low the sur-face of the wa-ter; and chim-neys, guards, and pi-lot hou-ses were swept a-way by the boughs that reached down from a-bove and stretched out on ei-ther side.

The men were kept at work night and day un-der the fire of reb-el guns, and on the 20th of March Por-ter was at-tacked by sharp-shoot-ers. His heav-y guns were not meant for war-fare in the woods, and if Sher-man did not come to his aid he felt that he would have to with-draw.

Sher-man—" old Te-cum-seh"—was then at the point where the Big Black *bay-ou* and the Deer Creek meet. He at once sent for-ward all the troops on hand, and when in a few hours oth-ers came up, al-though it was night, he marched at their head, a-long the nar-row and on-ly track of hard land that had been found, lead-ing his troops by can-dle light through the cane-brake.

Sher-man and his men soon drove off the reb-el skir-mish-ers, and saved the Ad-mi-ral and his fleet. Por-ter found, how-ev-er, that there was no chance of his get-ting his boats past the block-ade which the reb-els had set up fur-ther on, and which was guard-ed by a strong force of troops, and as there was no land route, gun-boats, i-ron clads, and trans-ports had to turn back, just as they were near the Ya-zoo Riv-er, and the scheme was giv-en up.

In the Fall of 1861 the North sought to get Mo-bile, New Or-le-ans and Tex-as out of reb-el hands, and to that end placed Gen-er-al B. F. But-ler in com-mand of what was called the De-part-ment of the Gulf. When But-ler took his or-ders from the men at Wash-ing-ton, he said to Mr. Lin-coln:

"Good-bye, Mr. Pres-i-dent; we shall take New Or-le-ans, or you will nev-er see me a-gain."

Sec-re-ta-ry of War Stan-ton, said to him, "The man who takes New Or-le-ans is made Lieu-ten-ant-gen-er-al."

But-ler left Hamp-ton Roads on the 25th of Feb-ru-a-ry, with his wife, his staff, and 1,400 troops, in the fine steam-ship MIS-SIS-SIP-PI. They passed through fear-ful storms, and at the end of a month reached Ship Isl-and, off the coast of Mis-sis-sip-pi, where both na-val and land for-ces met, and made their plans for at-tack. Here were Com-mo-dores Far-ra-gut and Por-ter with a mor-tar fleet of 20 schoon-ers, each with a mor-tar that weighed eight and a half tons, and could throw a 15-inch shell that weighed, when filled, 212 pounds. Each ves-sel was al-so armed with two 32-pound-ers, and the whole force was in first-rate trim.

The reb-els had two forts, Jack-son and St. Phil-ip, one on each side of the Mis-sis-sip-pi, 75 miles from its five mouths that o-pen in-to the Gulf of Mex-i-co, which they had made as strong as they could. Near them lay a fleet of 13 gun-boats, an i-ron clad float-ing fort, and the great reb-el ram MA-NAS-SAS.

The reb-els had built this queer kind of a gun-boat at New Or-le-ans, and called it a "ram," be-cause it had a

THE RAM MA-NAS-SAS.

strong i-ron beak on its bow, for fierce push-ing. This mon-ster was com-mand-ed by J. S. Hol-lins, late of the U-ni-ted States Na-vy, and in the fall of 1861 was sent to the South West Pass of the Mis-sis-sip-pi Riv-er, to at-tack a small block-ade that was there. It made a fierce as-sault, and in the hands of a man of more skill might have done a great deal of harm; but it did no more than punch a hole in the side of the gun-boat RICH-MOND, wound a schoon-er, sink a boat, and stave in the long light boat, known as the "gig." The fear that the reb-els might send down more such mon-sters, made the men at Wash-ing-ton speed their plans for the cap-ture of New Or-le-ans.

IV.—PASSING THE FORTS BELOW NEW ORLEANS.

On the 16th of A-pril the fleet dropped anch-or on the west bank of the stream, and the next day the ships were stripped of all that would be in their way when they went in-to bat-tle. Spars, boats, sails, and ropes were sent on shore, and all things made snug and taut a-round the masts.

Some of the ships had their hulls daubed with mud—of which there is no lack in the Mis-sis-sip-pi Riv-er—and their spars and rig-ging decked with boughs, so that at night the reb-els would think them a part of the shore.

MOR-TER BOATS COV-ERED WITH BOUGHS.

Fort Jack-son o-pened fire on the 18th, and then a storm of bomb-shells was sent from Por-ter's fleet, and this was kept up for some days.

Each night the reb-els sent down fire-rafts, which did no great harm to the ships, as the crews in their boats towed them a-shore, or the light steam-ers ran up and put them out with their hose.

FIRE RAFTS.

But though mor-tar boats and gun-boats kept up their fire of shot and shell, the forts still stood, and as Far-ra-gut saw no way in which they could be brought down, he made up his mind to run by them with his fleet.

But this was no slight task, for on the right and left banks of the river were rafts of large trees, held in place with great i-ron chains. Two gun-boats, the I-TAS-CA and the PI-NO-LA, were sent out to break up this block-ade of rafts. They set out on a dark night, and as their masts were out and their hulls set low in the wa-ter, they could scarce have been seen by the reb-els, and all might have gone well from the start had the tide not been so swift.

Two or three tri-als were made by both boats, and then the I-TAS-CA went a-ground, hard and fast with-in range of both forts. Word was at once sent to the PI-NO-LA, which was so long on the way that the I-TAS-CA was in great fear that she had been left to her fate. It was near the hour when the moon would rise, and there was no time to lose. The PI-NO-LA came up af-ter a while, and fixed a great tow-line to the I-TAS-CA, and by dint of long pulls and strong pulls, made out to drag the boat out of the mud, and swing her out in-to the riv-er, with her head up stream. As soon as Lieu-ten-ant Cald-well found that his ship was a-float, he put on steam and went a-head at full speed. The tide was with the boat and as she came up to the rafts—or "hulks," as sea-men called them—Cald-well cried "star-board!" and the I-TAS-CA steered straight for the chains. They snapped—the I-TAS-CA went through—and the riv-er was free!

The bom-bard-ment be-gan on the 18th of A-pril, the mor-tar boats ta-king the lead, with or-ders to fire a bomb-shell ev-er-y ten min-utes. The gun-boats ran up now and then to draw the en-e-my's fire, or to give aid to the mor-tar boats.

On the first day Fort Jack-son was set on fire and burned un-til two o'clock the next morn-ing. Cloth-ing and oth-er val-u-a-ble goods were burnt up, and much suf-fer-ing was caused by the in-tense heat.

Dur-ing the night the fi-ring ceased on both sides. A mor-tar schoon-er was sunk by a ri-fle shell that struck the deck, and went down through the bot-tom of the ves-sel, but near-ly all her arms and stores were saved. One or two men were wound-ed, but lit-tle oth-er dam-age was done ex-cept to the masts and rig-ging of some of the schoon-ers.

The reb-els fared much worse, and the fire with-in and with-out soon made Fort Jack-son look like a ru-ined and de-sert-ed cit-a-del.

As the soil was wet and soft, the bomb-shells made holes in the ground, 18 or 20 feet deep, and then burst with a noise like an earth-quake.

The le-vee, or em-bank-ment, was bro-ken so that the wa-ter rushed in-to the fort, and flood-ed the pa-rade ground and case-mates.

A case-mate is a bomb-proof space in which can-non may be placed, to be fired through an em-bra-sure or o-pen-ing.

It is some-times used as a store-room, or mag-a-zine

(*zeen*), for pow-der, shot, shells, and oth-er in-stru-ments of war-fare, and troops may al-so be placed there.

At two o'clock on the morn-ing of the 24th of A-pril, Far-ra-gut weighed anch-or and set out to-ward New Or-le-ans. The fleet was cut in-to three parts. The flag-ship HART-FORD, the RICH-MOND, and the BROOK-LYN were to keep near the right bank of the riv-er to fight Fort Jack-son.

The PEN-SA-CO-LA, MIS-SIS-SIP-PI, VA-RU-NA, KA-TAH-DIN, KIN-E-O, WIS-SA-HICK-ON and PORTS-MOUTH were to hug the left bank, and to fight Fort St. Phil-ip. These were in com-mand of Cap-tain The-o-do-rus Bai-ley, whose flag-ship was the CAY-U-GA.

Cap-tain Bell was to keep in mid-stream with the SCI-O-TO, WI-NO-NA, IR-O-QUOIS, PIN-O-LA, I-TAS-CA and KEN-NE-BEC.

The CAY-U-GA passed through the hulks with-out harm, and close be-hind her came the PEN-SA-CO-LA, which stopped, when near Fort St. Phil-ip, to pour a broad-side that drove the reb-el gun-ners from the works on top of the par-a-pet.

As the big ship went by at a slow rate of speed, the gun-ners came back to their guns and fired at her a-gain. The PEN-SA-CO-LA stopped, and once more her fierce fire drove off the gun-ners, and when they came back and the ship was too far up the stream for her guns to bear, they turned their fire on her, and rid-dled her well.

Then the reb-el ram, MA-NAS-SAS, bore down the stream and charged the PEN-SA-CO-LA, which was swung a-bout so that she did not get the thrust that was meant for her, and sent a broad-side from star-board in-to the ram, which steamed on down past the U-ni-on fleet whose shot, from right and left, went through her sides as though they were paste-board.

The MIS-SIS-SIP-PI came up in the rear of the PEN-SA-CO-LA, at a slow rate of speed, so as to keep out of range of her guns, and made an at-tack on Fort St. Phil-ip.

Just at this time the reb-el ram struck her on the port side, and gave her a jar that made her feel as if she had gone a-ground, and a wound in her side sev-en feet long and four inch-es deep. Then the tide caught her, and swung her a-cross the stream to the Fort Jack-son side.

All of Cap-tain Bai-ley's boats made out to pass the forts, but Cap-tain Bell did not have as good luck. The night was dark, the tide was strong, and they were borne first to this side and then to that, and found it hard to keep track of the space be-tween the ships.

Far-ra-gut in the fore-chains, with night-glass in hand,

kept close watch on all that took place. As the HART-FORD steered in to-ward Fort Jack-son, a fire-raft came down on her and caused her to sheer right a-cross the riv-er, where she went a-ground near Fort St. Phil-ip. A small tug, with a crew of six men, drove the fire-raft close up to the big ship HART-FORD, and in the bright light of the fire made her a shi-ning mark for the guns in the forts. A shot from the big ship went through the heart of the small tug, and she and the brave men on board of her, sank to the bot-tom of the MIS-SIS-SIP-PI.

THE HART-FORD A-GROUND.

The HART-FORD was soon a mass of flame on her port side half way up to the main top, and the crew had to work hard to save their ship, which was now be-tween three fires. Both forts fired on her, and the guns of the Hart-ford gave back shot for shot, un-til at last she worked her-self clear, and passed out of their range.

Ere the ves-sels had got well a-way from the forts, the reb-el rams and gun-boats took part in the fight, and the scene was a grand one.

The Cay-u-ga, when a-bout five miles a-bove the forts, came on a reb-el camp on the right bank of the riv-er. Shots were fired, and in a few mo-ments the troops laid down their arms, and be-came pris-on-ers of war.

The Ma-nas-sas had kept in the rear of the U-ni-on fleet, but, when she came near, the Mis-sis-sip-pi turned on her, drove her a-shore, poured two broad-sides in-to her and left her a wreck. In a short time she slipped off the bank, and went down past the forts, a mass of

BURN-ING OF THE MA-NAS-SAS.

flames. As she passed Por-ter's mor-tar boats, which were still be-low the forts, some of them tried to get hold of her, but ere it could be done, her one big gun burst, and she sank to the bot-tom of the riv-er.

All this, and more than can be told by tongue or pen, went on in the dark hours of the night, and in the space of an hour and a half the U-ni-on ves-sels had passed both forts, and the great bat-tle was fought, in which the reb-els lost al-most the whole of their fleet.

But-ler in the mean-time had put some of his troops on shore be-low the forts, and these, led by a man who knew the route through the bay-ous, made their way to the rear of Fort Phil-ip. Some were sent a-bove Fort Jack-son, and as Por-ter kept up a fire of bomb-shells, the reb-els—as-sailed in front and rear—gave up the fight, ran up the white flag, and 1,000 men laid down their arms, and marched out as pris-on-ers.

CHAPTER VIII.

OFF NEW OR-LE-ANS AND VICKS-BURG.

With the nine ves-sels that he had left, Far-ra-gut pushed on to-ward New Or-le-ans; and the news that the U-ni-on fleet was near caused a reign of ter-ror in the streets of the "Cres-cent Cit-y."

Ships and steam-boats were burned at their wharves. Ships on fire, load-ed with cot-ton, float-ed down the stream, and the whole con-tents of great ship-yards were sent a-drift so that they could be of no use to the vic-tors.

The reb-el troops fled from their posts. Men of means left their homes and their stores. Wo-men ran through the streets bare-head-ed, and with pis-tols in their hands.

Shouts and screams rent the air, and cries of "Burn the cit-y! Nev-er mind us! Burn the cit-y!" were heard on all sides.

A storm came up, and the thun-der and light-ning joined in to add to the wild-ness of the scene, and in the midst of it all, at one o'clock in the af-ter-noon of A-pril 25, 1862, the squad-ron dropped anch-or in front of New Or-le-ans.

The sail-ors gave a cheer. Some un-wise per-sons on shore cheered back. Pis-tol shots were at once fired at these by the ex-cited crowd, and quite a num-ber of folks were wound-ed.

Far-ra-gut sent Cap-tain Bai-ley on shore with a flag of truce, to de-mand the sur-ren-der of the cit-y.

He and Lieu-ten-ant Per-kins, who went with him, were met with scorn and rage by the mob, who shook

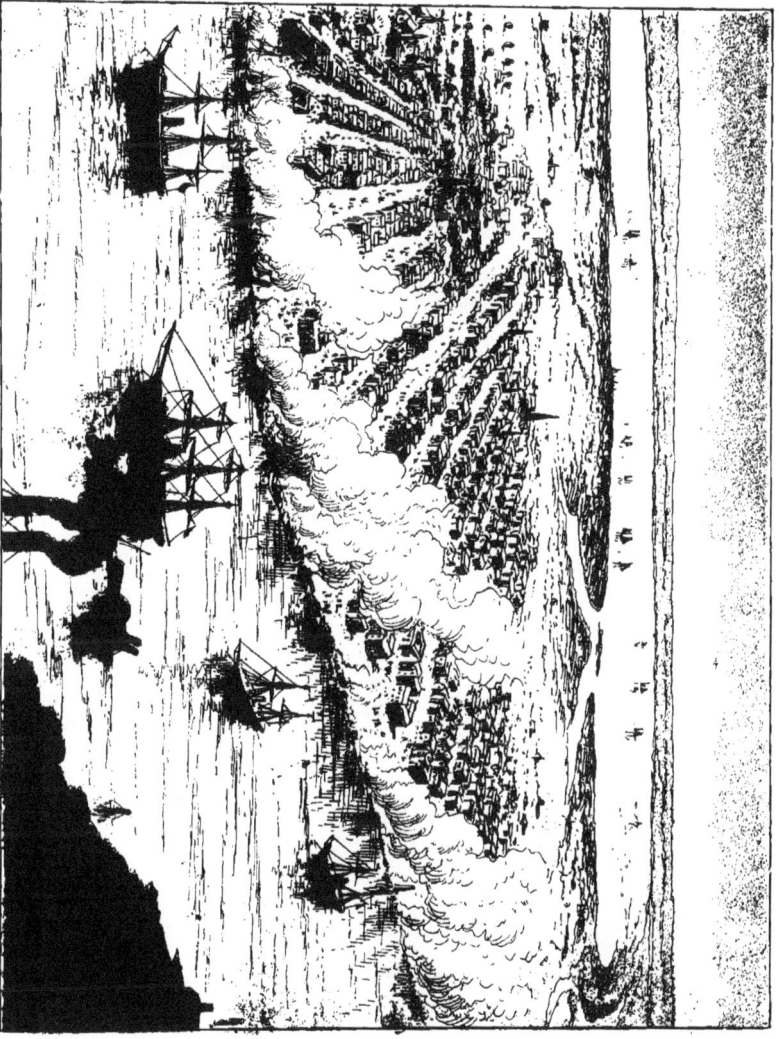

V.—CAPTURE OF NEW ORLEANS.

their fists in the fa-ces of the two brave men, and cried out "Choke them! Give them rot-ten eggs!"

It was then de-cid-ed that Cap-tain Bai-ley should re-turn to the fleet, un-til it could be found out what the May-or and Com-mon Coun-cil meant to do.

Then the brave Cap-tain Bell stepped forth, and be-sought Far-ra-gut to let him take the ma-rines (*may-reens*) —sol-diers trained to serve on ship-board—and plant the U-ni-on flag on all the Gov-ern-ment build-ings. To this Far-ra-gut gave his con-sent, and this hand-ful of men was soon lost sight of in the howl-ing mob.

But it was not long be-fore the U-ni-on flag was seen fly-ing from the Cit-y Hall, and at sight of it cheers went up from the U-ni-on fleet, and howls of rage from the crowd at the doors.

The May-or is the chief mag-is-trate; and he and the Com-mon Coun-cil make the laws that gov-ern towns and cit-ies.

Far-ra-gut sent the May-or a let-ter which read some-what like this:

"U. S. FLAG SHIP HART-FORD, OFF NEW OR-LE-ANS,
A-pril 26, 1862.

"*To his Ex-cel-len-cy, the May-or of New Or-le-ans:*

"SIR: On my ar-ri-val be-fore your cit-y I had the

hon-or to send to your hon-or Cap-tain Bai-ley, U. S. N., to de-mand of you the sur-ren-der of New Or-le-ans. Cap-tain Bai-ley re-port-ed the re-sult of an in-ter-view with your-self and the mil-i-ta-ry pow-ers. Your hon-or must know that a na-val of-fi-cer can-not take up-on him-self the du-ties of a mil-i-ta-ry com-man-dant. I came here to force New Or-le-ans to o-bey the laws of the Gov-ern-ment of the U-ni-ted States, and to a-venge its in-sult-ed ma-jest-y.

"The rights of per-sons and prop-er-ty shall be se-cured. I there-fore de-mand of you the sur-ren-der of the cit-y, and that the em-blem of the sov-er-eign-ty of the U-ni-ted States be hoist-ed o-ver the Cit-y Hall, Mint, and Cus-tom House by noon this day; and that all flags and oth-er em-blems of sov-er-eign-ty than those of the U-ni-ted States, be re-moved from all the pub-lic build-ings at that hour.

"I fur-ther re-quest that you shall use your pow-er to quell dis-turb-an-ces, re-store or-der, and call on all the good peo-ple of New Or-le-ans to re-turn at once to their pur-suits; and I de-mand that no per-son shall be harmed in per-son or prop-er-ty be-cause of their loy-al-ty to the Gov-ern-ment.

"I shall speed-i-ly and se-vere-ly pun-ish a-ny per-son or

per-sons who shall com-mit such out-ra-ges as were seen yes-ter-day, when armed men fired up-on help-less wo-men and chil-dren for giv-ing ex-pres-sion to their pleas-ure at see-ing the old flag.

"I am, ver-y re-spect-ful-ly,

D. G. FAR-RA-GUT,

Flag-Of-fi-cer West-ern Gulf Squad-ron."

The May-or re-fused to sur-ren-der, or to haul down the flag of Lou-i-si-an-a from the Cit-y Hall, and this called forth oth-er let-ters from Far-ra-gut, one of which reads thus:

"U. S. FLAG SHIP HART-FORD, at anch-or, off the Cit-y of New Or-le-ans, A-pril 28, 1862.

"To His Hon-or, the May-or and Com-mon Coun-cil of the Cit-y of New Or-le-ans:

"Your let-ters of the 26th have been re-ceived.

"I deep-ly re-gret to see both by their con-tents, and the dis-play of the flag of Lou-i-si-an-a on the Court House, a de-ter-mi-na-tion on your part not to haul it down. More-o-ver, when my of-fi-cers and men were sent on shore to con-sult with those in pow-er, and to hoist the U-ni-ted States flag on the Cus-tom House, with strict or-ders not to use their arms un-less as-sailed, they were in-sult-ed in the gross-est man-ner, and the flag which had been hoist-ed by my or-ders on the Mint was pulled down and dragged through the streets.

"All of which goes to show that the fire of this fleet may be drawn up-on the cit-y at a-ny mo-ment, and in such an e-vent the le-vee would be cut by the shells, and cause an im-mense a-mount of dis-tress to the in-no-cent pop-u-la-tion, which I as-sure you that I de-sire by all means to a-void.

"The choice re-mains with you. But it be-comes my du-ty to no-ti-fy you to re-move the wo-men and chil-dren from the cit-y with-in for-ty-eight hours, if I right-ly un-der-stood your de-ter-mi-na-tion.

"Very re-spect-ful-ly, your o-be-di-ent ser-vant,

D. G. FAR-RA-GUT,
Flag Of-fi-cer, West-ern Gulf Block-a-ding Squad-ron."

Far-ra-gut was not a harsh man, and it grieved him to have to turn his guns on the cit-y, but such were the rules of war, and it was his du-ty to o-bey them. The May-or sent him a spite-ful let-ter, char-ging him with a de-sire to mur-der help-less wo-men and chil-dren, which so shocked the ten-der heart-ed man that he would have no-thing more to say to May-or Mon-roe, but made up his mind to wait for Gen-er-al But-ler, and to turn the cit-y o-ver to him and his troops.

But-ler's troops came on the e-ven-ing of May 1, and New Or-le-ans was placed in their care with the U-ni-ted States flag fly-ing at high mast. But-ler at once gave or-ders that car-goes of flour, live stock, and oth-er stores should be brought from Mo-bile and pla-ces in-land, to sup-ply the need of the peo-ple in New Or-le-ans where there was great dis-tress.

Large as was the sup-ply it did not meet the de-mand, and that all might have a share, though a small one, But-ler sent out an or-der—or proc-la-ma-tion as it is called—which, though rath-er long, is well worth read-ing.

"*Head-quar-ters De-part-ment of the Gulf,*
New Or-le-ans, May 9, 1862.

"The sad state of want and hun-ger of the me-chan-ics and work-ing class-es in this cit-y, has been made known to the com-mand-ing gen-er-al.

"He has act-ed on the ad-vice of the cit-y gov-ern-ment in fur-nish-ing food to the poor of New Or-le-ans, but no re-lief has as yet been af-ford-ed by them.

"This hun-ger does not pinch the rich and pow-er-ful, the lead-ers of the re-bell-ion, who have got-ten up this war, and are now stri-ving to car-ry it on with-out re-gard to the starv-ing poor, the work-ing man, his wife and child. Un-mind-ful of their suf-fer-ing fel-low cit-i-zens at home, they have caused or al-lowed pro-vis-ions to be ta-ken out of the cit-y for Con-fed-er-ate ser-vice, since New Or-le-ans has been oc-cu-pied by the U-ni-ted States for-ces.

"La-fay-ette Square, their home of wealth, was made the dé-pót (*day-po*) of mil-i-ta-ry stores, and not of pro-vis-ions for their poor neigh-bors. Strik-ing hands with the vile, the gam-bler, the i-dler, and the ruf-fi-an, they have de-stroyed the su-gar and cot-ton, which might have been ex-changed for food for the in-dus-tri-ous and good.

"They have be-trayed their coun-try. They have been false to e-ve-ry trust.

"They have shown them-selves in-ca-pa-ble of de-fend-ing the State they have seized up-on.

"They can-not pro-tect those they have ru-ined, but have left them to the mer-cies and mur-ders of a chron-ic mob.

"They will not feed those whom they are starv-ing.

"Most-ly with-out prop-er-ty them-selves, they have sto-len and de-stroyed the means of those who had prop-er-ty, leav-ing chil-dren pen-ni-less and old age hope-less.

"Men of Lou-i-si-an-a, work-ing men, prop-er-ty hold-ers, mer-chants and cit-i-zens of the U-ni-ted States, of what-ev-er na-tion you may have had birth, how long will you up-hold these wrongs, and suf-fer your-selves to be made the serfs of these lead-ers?

"The U-ni-ted States has sent land and na-val for-ces here, to fight and sub-due the reb-el ar-mies in ar-ray a-gainst her au-thor-i-ty.

"We find flee-ing mass-es, run-a-way prop-er-ty own-ers, a whis-key drink-ing mob, and starv-ing cit-i-zens with their wives and chil-dren. It is our du-ty to call back the first, to pun-ish the sec-ond, root out the third, feed and pro-tect the last. We had not pre-pared our-selves to pro-vide food for the hun-gry and dis-tressed, but to the ex-tent pos-si-ble with-in the pow-er of the com-mand-ing gen-er-al it shall be done.

"He has seized a quan-ti-ty of beef and su-gar in-tend-ed for the reb-els in the field. A thou-sand bar-rels of those stores will be dealt out a-mong the de-serv-ing poor of this cit-y, from whom the reb-els had sto-len it; e-ven al-though some of the food will go to sup-ply the cra-ving wants of the wives and chil-dren of those now herd-ing at Camp Moore and else-where, in arms a-gainst the U-ni-ted States.

"Cap-tain John Clark, act-ing Chief Com-mis-sa-ry of Sub-sis-tence, will see that this or-der is car-ried out, and will give pub-lic no-tice of the place and man-ner of dis-tri-bu-tion, which will be ar-ranged as far as pos-si-ble, so that the un-worth-y and dis-or-der-ly will not share in its ben-e-fits.

"By com-mand of Ma-jor Gen-er-al But-ler."
"George C. Strong, As-sis-tant Ad-ju-tant Gen-er-al, Chief of Staff."

By prompt, and oft-times se-vere ex-er-cise of the rules of mil-i-ta-ry law, Gen-er-al But-ler made out to pre-serve some-thing like or-der in the Cit-y of New Or-le-ans.

Strict rules were laid down, ar-rests were made, and all cit-i-zens, wheth-er male or fe-male, were com-pelled to be-have them-selves, and to re-spect the U-ni-ted States troops, as well as the U-ni-ted States flag.

These acts caused a great deal of bit-ter feel-ing a-mong the reb-els in New Or-le-ans, and those in the field, and some of Gen-er-al But-ler's or-ders gave so much of-fence, that Ma-jor Gen-er-al Banks was sent to take his place.

E-ven this did not bring peace, and on Christ-mas Day, 1862, men cheered for Jeff Da-vis in the pub-lic streets of New Or-le-ans, and used threats a-gainst the mil-i-ta-ry, whose du-ty it was to put down ri-ots and ri-ot-ers.

Far-ra-gut, af-ter he left New Or-le-ans in But-ler's hands, kept his fleet at work on the Mis-sis-sip-pi—took Bat-on Rouge—and on June 26 was in front of Vicks-burg. There were great strong-holds there, manned by the reb-el troops that fled from New Or-le-ans, and they were up too high to be much hurt by the guns of the squad-ron. There were no pi-lots to guide the ships, so they kept close to the shore on the town side, and at day-light on the 28th the HART-FORD and six of her fleet ran by the forts, un-der cov-er of the fire of the mor-tar boats which had come up to their aid. It was well known that Vicks-burg would have to be ta-ken and held by a land force, but it had been said that our boats could not pass the reb-el forts at this place, and the head men at Wash-ing-ton thought they would like to put it to the test.

If the thing could be done Far-ra-gut was the man to do it, and he ran past the forts, gave Grant a chance to get to Gen-er-al Banks, and on the 28th of July took his fleet back to New Or-le-ans, which was 100 miles be-low Vicks-burg.

PASS-ING THE BAT-TE-RIES AT VICKS-BURG.

For the next year or two Far-ra-gut spent the most of his time on the sea-board, and Ad-mi-ral Por-ter had charge of the Mis-sis-sip-pi Squad-ron which gave great aid to Gen-er-al Grant. In the mean-time, the reb-els had built the mon-ster "ram" AR-KAN-SAS, which was to drive the Yan-kees from New Or-le-ans. Three of our gun-boats went out to meet her, but some-how the "ram" did not work well, and at last her com-mand-er ran her on shore and set her on fire.

En-gland had shown her-self such a good friend to the South, that the reb-els had a Brit-ish ship-builder build ves-sels for them to use as pri-va-teers.

VI.—THE FIGHT OF THE KEAR-SARGE AND A-LA-BA-MA.

The first one, the O-RE-TO, was sent to sea in dis-guise, sailed for the port of Nas-sau, and in the fall of 1862 was seen off Mo-bile, fly-ing the Brit-ish flag. She ran in-to that har-bor, passed the block-a-ding fleet, and ran out a-gain in De-cem-ber, when she bore the name of FLOR-I-DA.

THE AL-A BA MA BURN-ING SHIPS.

She kept on the coast for some time, and al-though the U-ni-on ves-sels kept a close watch on her she was too sharp for them, and made out to do much harm to the North. She was seized at last and sunk at New-port News.

The most fa-mous of the cruis-ers was the AL-A-BA-MA in com-mand of Cap-tain Ra-pha-el Semmes. She was built at Liv-er-pool, sailed from a Brit-ish port, and bore the Brit-ish flag, and for a year and a half she kept the sea in a blaze of light from the U-ni-on ships she seized and fired. Men told of her deeds with blanched fa-ces, and the name of Semmes took rank with that of the pi-rate of old, the fa-mous Cap-tain Kidd.

Late in the spring of 1864, the AL-A-BA-MA lay up at Cher-bourg, a port on the coast of France, and in June she was found there by the U-ni-ted States steam-ship KEAR-SARGE, com-mand-ed by Cap-tain J. A. Wins-low.

On Sun-day, the 19th of June, the AL-A-BA-MA, well armed, went out to fight the KEAR-SARGE.

A yacht kept near to give aid to Semmes, and to snatch him and his of-fi-cers and to bear them in safe-ty to En-gland, in case the KEAR-SARGE should win the fight.

As soon as the two ves-sels were well out on the high sea—their law-ful bat-tle field—they be-gan the fight at long range, and for an hour moved round and round fir-ing their guns at each turn.

The AL-A-BA-MA was hurt, and her flag went down; but Wins-low was not sure that it was a sur-ren-der, as the ropes might have been shot a-way. Then a white flag was thrown o-ver the stern, and the guns of the KEAR-SARGE at once ceased their fire. But the foe had

VII.—THE SINKING OF THE A-LA-BA-MA.

the heart of a Ben-e-dict Ar-nold, and in a few min-utes sent two shots at the KEAR-SARGE, and tried to run back in-to Cher-bourg, where Wins-low would have no right to touch her.

This act brought on her a fierce fire from the KEAR-SARGE, which made the AL-A-BA-MA plead for mer-cy in real ear-nest, for the sea rushed in through the great gaps made by the U-ni-on shot.

As the AL-A-BA-MA went down Wins-low did his best to save the crew, and took off 65 of them. The En-glish yacht picked up Semmes and his of-fi-cers and a few men, and bore them to En-gland out of harm's way, and a great deal was made of them.

It took a long time to set-tle this af-fair be-tween En-gland and A-mer-i-ca, and the North felt quite sore at the way it had been served. Wise men from both sides met to de-cide the case, and En-gland had to pay $15,500,000 in gold for the dam-age that was done by Semmes, the great sea-rover.

THE CHAIN AR-MOR OF THE KEAR-SARGE.

Rams, gun-boats, and mor-tar boats kept up their raids on the Mis-sis-sip-pi, and Por-ter made use of all sorts of de-vi-ces to scare the reb-els, who were in force on the riv-er 'twixt Vicks-burg and Port Hud-son.

One night he sent down a raft fixed up to look like a ram, with smoke stacks made of pork-bar-rels. On the sides were paint-ed in large let-ters " De-lu-ded peo-ple

THE COM-IC RAM.

cave in." There was no one on board of her, and as she passed the forts at Vicks-burg the reb-els fired on her, but she kept right on her way.

The reb-els be-low Vicks-burg were in such dread of this queer mon-ster, that they blew up the IN-DI-AN-O-LA, and her great guns sank to the bot-tom of the riv-er.

Far-ra-gut had heard of what was go-ing on in the Mis-sis-sip-pi, and made up his mind to run by the reb-el bluffs at Port Hud-son, and place the riv-er from that point to Vicks-burg once more in U-ni-on hands.

It was a dark night in the month of March, 1863, that Far-ra-gut set out on this trip, in the flag-ship HART-FORD, with a gun-boat lashed to her side. The rest of the large ves-sels came in her wake each with a gun-boat lashed to her side. When the fleet came in range of forts on the bluffs, the reb-els sent at them a most ter-ri-fic show-er of shot, shells, and bul-lets from all the guns that could be brought to bear on them.

THE FIGHT AT PORT HUD-SON.

The guns of the fleet spoke back, but were too low down to do much harm. For an hour and a half the fierce fire was kept up, then it ceased; and but two of the fleet, the HART-FORD and her gun-boat, had passed Port Hud-son.

The M<small>IS-SIS-SIP-PI</small> ran a-ground and was set on fire, and the rest of the war-ships went back be-low Port Hud-son.

Late in May Far-ra-gut went to aid Banks in an at-tack on Port Hud-son, and with the H<small>ART-FORD</small> and the A<small>L-BA-TROSS</small>, and one or two more gun-boats a-bove Port Hud-son, and the M<small>O-NON-GA-HE-LA</small>, R<small>ICH-MOND</small>, E<small>S-SEX</small> and G<small>EN-E-SEE</small>, with the mor-tar boats be-low, he poured a stream of shells in-to the fort.

There was not much chance for the reb-els be-tween Banks's and Far-ra-gut's great guns, but they kept up the fight un-til the 9th of Ju-ly, when they raised the white flag and gave more than 6,000 troops in-to U-ni-on hands.

MOR-TAR BOATS.

Ere this date Vicks-burg had been forced to sur-ren-der to Grant, and the Mis-sis-sip-pi was once more free from St. Lou-is to New Or-le-ans.

CHAPTER IX.

UP THE RED RIV-ER.

As the Mis-sis-sip-pi, with its chief ports had been wrenched from the hands of the reb-els, Mo-bile and Tex-as were the two points next to be at-tacked.

Gen-er-al Banks, who was now in com-mand of the De-part-ment of the Gulf, had a mind to move up-on Mo-bile at once, as the reb-els were in force at that place and had done much to add to its strength.

But the Em-per-or of France, Na-po-le-on III. had not shown him-self a good friend of the U-ni-ted States, and when on the 10th of June the French ar-my came in-to Mex-i-co, Banks had or-ders to change his course, but it was not till Sep-tem-ber that the troops were un-der way.

Gen-er-al Hal-leck wished to have Banks and his force move up the Red Riv-er, but left it to him to de-cide which was the best course to take. The Red Riv-er was so low that boats could not get up it, and so Banks made up his mind to work on the sea-coast, and make his first at-tack on Sa-bine Pass and the town near it. If he got a foot-hold here he could march on to Beaumont, and thence to Hous-ton, the chief town of Tex-as, ere the reb-els could get them-selves in trim to drive him back.

At that time the West Gulf Squad-ron was in com-mand of Com-mo-dore Hen-ry H. Bell, who was forced to choose gun-boats of light weight and small draught, as they a-lone could cross the bar. On the 7th of Sep-tem-ber, the gun-boats and trans-ports crossed the bar and dropped anch-or two miles from the fort, and the CLIF-TON, SA-CHEM AND A-RI-ZO-NA be-gan at once to at-tack the works.

In half an hour a shot from the fort pierced the SA-CHEM so that she had to give up the fight, and in a few mo-ments the CLIF-TON was struck, and both boats hauled down their flags. They lost 39 men, most of whom were drowned, and as the plan had been to sur-prise the foe, this route was giv-en up, and the gun-boats and trans-ports were with-drawn on the night of the 7th.

Banks' next scheme was to land at the far end of the Tex-as coast line, near the Ri-o Gran-de and work his way to the East; and on the 26th of Oc-to-ber a force of 3,500 men, in com-mand of Gen-er-al Da-na, sailed from New Or-le-ans, and Banks went with it.

The foe gave way be-fore the U-ni-on troops, the

THE FIGHT AT SA-BINE PASS.

U-ni-ted States flag was raised in Tex-as, and all went well un-til they came near Gal-ves-ton, where the reb-els were in force. Banks felt that his next move must be to-ward their rear, but he could not make an at-tack there un-less he had more troops, and the aid of the Mis-sis-sip-pi squad-ron.

Sher-man sent word to Banks that he would lend him 10,000 men, and Ad-mi-ral Por-ter said he would go with him up the Red Riv-er, with a large force of gun-boats. Por-ter did not think much of Banks' scheme, as it was sure to fail, but Banks urged him to join him, and said if he did not go, and it failed, he would be to blame, and when he put it in this way Por-ter felt that he must lend his aid.

The Red Riv-er takes its name from the col-or of its

wa-ter. In some parts of its course it is half a mile wide, and at low tide is but four feet deep. In some pla-ces the banks are quite high, and the stream is so crook-ed and so nar-row here and there, that it is no light task to get ves-sels through at the best of times.

The rise in the riv-er did not be-gin un-til De-cem-ber, and there would not be wa-ter e-nough so that the gun-boats and trans-ports could pass the Falls of Al-ex-an-dri-a, be-fore the spring rise in March. This year it chanced that the riv-er was more back-ward than it had been in twen-ty years, and it was late in March ere the ves-sels could start.

Banks and his own troops marched by land to Natch-i-to-ches, and Ad-mi-ral Por-ter set out with fif-teen gun-boats, three light steam-boats, and trans-ports filled with troops from Sher-man's ar-my. The Red Riv-er was full of logs, and a great deal of time had to be spent by the gun-boats in drag-ging them out of the mud, and send-ing them down stream so that they would drift out in-to the Mis-sis-sip-pi. These de-lays kept back the ves-sels so that they were too late to aid in the at-tack on Fort de Rus-sy, which was made by A. J. Smith.

As the flo-til-la came with-in two miles of the place they could hear the sound of the guns, and as they turned a point with the gun-boats a mile from the fort, they could see the rain of shot and shell poured in by the U-ni-on troops, on those who sought to screen themselves be-hind the earth-works.

AT-TACK ON FORT DE RUS-SY.

Por-ter had hoped to take part in the fight, but Gen-er-al Smith did not need him, and the flo-til-la pushed on to Al-ex-an-dri-a, while Smith staid be-hind to pull down Fort de Rus-sy. He said he would show the reb-els that though they could build the strong-est forts in the world, the U-ni-on men were strong e-nough to pull them down, and he did not mean to leave one stone on an-oth-er. He kept at it for three days, and then gave it up as a bad job, and went on to Al-ex-an-dri-a.

Por-ter says, "When Gen-er-al Smith joined me at

the mouth of the riv-er with his di-vis-i-on, he had, I be-lieve, just come off a long march. The clothes of his men were worn and fa-ded, their shoes were patched, they had no tents to sleep un-der, though they may have had blank-ets." Their tents were on the trans-ports, and the gen-er-al would not have them used with-out his or-ders. He had been heard to call an of-fi-cer a "Miss Nan-cy kind of a fel-low," be-cause he slept un-der a shel-ter tent. "I could nev-er see the use of one my-self," says Por-ter; but Smith seemed to think there was too much style in it to suit his boys, whom he taught to scorn com-fort and de-spise dan-ger.

One day Smith came on board the Ad-mi-ral's flag-ship, the CRICK-ET, and asked for a pair of leg i-rons. One of his men had not o-beyed or-ders and he want-ed to pun-ish him. "Why don't you 'buck' him," said Por-ter, "if he has been ve-ry bad?"

BUCK-ING.

Buck-ing is a pun-ish-ment made use of on ship-board. A stick is put un-der the sail-or's knees and made fast there with a rope. Then his

VIII.—THE START OF THE RED RIV-ER EX-PE-DI-TION.

hands are brought down and made fast to the stick, so that he can-not get up or sit down with ease. Some boys may have tried to play the game of mum-ble-peg when trussed in this way.

"Buck-ing is too good for him," said Smith. "He has dis-graced the whole com-mand. He is worse than a fe-lon, sir."

"Why, what has he done?" asked Por-ter. "It must be some-thing ver-y bad."

"Bad, sir, did you say? Well, I call it out-rage-ous. It's my hos-pi-tal stew-ard, and I found him sleep-ing out here un-der a tree on a camp cot! What do you think of that?"

HOS-PI-TAL STEW-ARD ON THE CAMP COT.

Por-ter laughed, and told Smith it was not worth while to pun-ish the boy so hard for so slight an of-fence, and said he'd bet-ter let him go, with a warn-ing.

"That I shall shoot him the next time," said Gen-er-al Smith.

When the flo-til-la reached Grand E-core, Ad-mi-ral Por-ter turned the flat-boats o-ver to Gen-er-al Banks, and then went on to-ward Shreve-port with the CRICK-ET, HIND-MAN, LEX-ING-TON, O-SAGE, NE-O-SHO, CHIL-LI-CO-THE, and the trans-ports with 2,500 troops on board.

They found the stream full of snags and sand-bars, and if they went the way the folks on the shore told them to go, they would find them-selves up a cut-off and have to turn back a-gain.

The Ad-mi-ral's flag-ship was a small stern-wheel boat, with a crew of 48 men and six six-pound-er boat-guns. He had room but for one horse, and some-thing ailed that one. He spoke of his need of a horse to Gor-ringe, who was then act-ing as flag cap-tain, and in less than three hours a fine black horse was brought up for the Ad-mi-ral's use.

AD-MI-RAL'S FLAG SHIP.

As he rode out that e-ven-ing he met the la-dy who owned the horse, who in a sneer-ing way asked him if he was en-joy-ing his ride, and if he would be kind e-nough to re-turn the horse be-fore he left the place.

The next day he rode down to the la-dy's house to thank her for the loan of her horse. She was on the porch as he rode up and came out to meet him, with a long sto-ry to tell a-bout "that old thief" the Ad-mi-ral whom she did not know by sight, but of whose deeds, she had heard.

Her slaves had raised her 22 bales of cot-ton, for which Kir-by Smith was to pay her ten cents a pound, and pass it through the U-ni-on lines for her. She would then have 1,320 dol-lars in U-ni-on mon-ey which she meant to change for Con-fed-er-ate scrip, and at the end of the war have a large for-tune to live on.

All boats in the Na-vy had or-ders to pick up all the bales of cot-ton that were found a-float, and land them in a North-ern port where they would be sold, and the mon-ey put in-to the U-ni-ted States Treas-u-ry. This was the law, and it was the du-ty of the Ad-mi-ral to see that it was kept by the Cap-tains and Com-mand-ers of all his fleet.

"But in comes that old skin-flint of an Ad-mi-ral," says she, "and sei-zes all my cot-ton, and hams, and sug-ar, and has them sent on board his ves-sel."

Por-ter said that it was strange, for the Ad-mi-ral gave strict or-ders to his men that they should not steal from pri-vate per-sons. "Do you know the name of the vessel and the cap-tain?" asked Por-ter.

She said she did, and gave them to him, and Por-ter told her that he knew the Ad-mi-ral well and would let him know of her case, and make her change her mind in re-gard to the "old skin-flint."

Por-ter sent word to the Cap-tain of the i-ron clad to re-turn the cot-ton, hams, and sug-ar at once, and gave him four hours to do it in. The goods were sent back, and Por-ter rode down the next day to see the la-dy. She saw him a long way off from the porch, and ran out to the gate to meet him.

"Oh, you dear good man!" said she, "I got all my things back; not a thing lost, thanks to you, and no thanks to that old cot-ton steal-er, your Ad-mi-ral. I know all a-bout him, and they say he steals cot-ton by the thou-sand bales at a time." She went on to say that she had a mind to give him that horse of hers, but he had been such a good friend to her that he was wor-thy a bet-ter steed, for to tell the truth, hers had seen its best days.

"I'll give you a horse fit for a king," said the la-dy.

"Sell him to me," said Por-ter; "I don't take gifts."

"I can't sell him," said Mrs. H—; "he isn't mine to

sell. He be-longs to one of our men who was wound-ed at Fort de Rus-sy. He is up-stairs now; and the horse is in my sta-ble. You can have him."

Por-ter said it would suit him best to use her horse as long as he staid there, and that was all the fa-vor he should ask.

"Oh, but there is one thing you must do," said Mrs. H—, as Por-ter was a-bout to take leave, "and that is to give me your name."

"If you will give me pen, ink and pa-per I will write it down for you," said he.

She ran off for these things, and when she brought them her guest wrote out his name in full—

"Ad-mi-ral Da-vid D. Por-ter, the great old rob-ber of the wid-ow and or-phan"—and gave it to her to read.

THE AD-MI-RAL WRI-TING HIS NAME.

Her face flushed a deep, deep red. "It can't be," she said in a husk-y voice. "Have I been such a fool as that?" and she sat down and had a good cry. Then she went out and brought the Ad-mi-ral a glass of milk, and said she was so a-shamed of her-self she could not talk. But she told the Ad-mi-ral some things he was glad to know, and he gave her ad-vice which she would not soon for-get.

Por-ter says that he was ri-ding out one day, when he saw a wo-man stand-ing on a house porch with her a-pron to her eyes. She was cry-ing and talk-ing to a sol-dier who held a large hen un-der his arm, " I thought there was some wrong do-ing go-ing on," says the Ad-mi-ral, "and so rode up to see what was the mat-ter. As I came up the wo-man took her a-pron from her eyes, which were full of tears."

"O Mr. Of-fi-cer!" she said, "won't you speak to this sol-dier and get him to give up my hen which he has ta-ken? She lays an egg ev-er-y day, and it is all the food my old mo-ther—who is 70 years old—can get in 24 hours. It is all she can eat. Do talk to him, and save our hen, and I will pray for you as long as I live!"

The Ad-mi-ral turned to the man and with an air of great stern-ness, said to him, "Well, you call your-self a sol-dier and can stand there un-moved when a wo-man in tears pleads to you for the hen on which her old mo-ther de-pends for her dai-ly food! You ought to be a-shamed to call your-self a U-ni-on sol-dier!"

The man looked up and smiled. "Do you hear me, or are you deaf?" asked the Ad-mi-ral.

"Yes, sir, I heard you," was the re-ply of the man, who was a real down-east Yan-kee, "and I've been think-ing of it. But Mr. Ad-mi-ral, I just want to put the case to you. Chick-ens will make soup and tears won't! Now that wo-man's tears ain't a bit of use to me, and this old hen is; it will make soup for our whole mess. All I've got to say is this: If you can make use of those tears you are wel-come to do so. All I've got to say a-gain is this: If you've got a dol-lar a-bout you and will give it to me, you can have this hen and give it to that wo-man, and she had bet-ter keep it locked up in a trunk, for there ain't man-y fel-lows you can trust in this ar-my."

"There's your dol-lar," said Por-ter; "give up the fowl, and prom-ise not to come here a-gain."

"Well, I'll do that, said the sol-dier, giv-ing the hen back to the wo-man whose tears were soon dried as she hugged her old friend to her breast, "but ma'am, may I ask the loan of your brush to get these feath-ers off my coat? If my mess-mates see feath-ers on me they will know I've been a-mong chick-ens—and I don't want to get bucked."

THE AD-MI-RAL AND THE HEN.

The man brushed himself with care and walked off quite cast down, because he had lost a chance for a taste of chick-en broth.

The men were so brave a-mid all the hardships of war, and their need of food was so great at times, that those in com-mand would not frown if they heard that they robbed hen-roosts and pig-pens, to get some-thing to take the place of salt pork and hard-tack.

Now we will go back to the boats a-gain which moved out of Al-ex-an-dri-a and wound their way to-ward Shreve-port. When the fleet drew near the mouth of the Shreve-port Riv-er, they found it blocked by a great steam-er that had been sunk there with her bow on one bank and her stern on the oth-er. To burn her would fill up the shoal spot where she lay, and to move her by piece-meal would take a long time.

The field guns were set on shore, and some of the of-fi-cers went out to look a-round. They saw some men run-ning in the high grass. Were they U-ni-on scouts or reb-el guer-ril-las? None knew for a fact; but Por-ter cried out "Banks has had a bat-tle and lost it!" and at once made haste to get the gun boats and trans-ports un-der way.

As they went down the stream they were fired on by

GUER-RIL-LAS AT-TACK-ING GUN BOATS.

sharp shoot-ers all a-long the banks, and had more than one sharp fight with the foe.

When Por-ter came near Grand E-core, where he thought that Banks and his men were, he found the ves-sels that had been sent a-head were stuck fast in the mud, and at the mer-cy of the sharp shoot-ers.

Por-ter passed through them in the CRICK-ET, and told the men to keep up their fire and he would send troops up to aid them. This he did, and at eight o'clock at night all the gun-boats and trans-ports were safe at Grand E-core—three hun-dred miles up the Red Riv-er, and in the land of foe-men.

As the Riv-er was fall-ing fast, Por-ter saw that it would not do to stay at Grand E-core, so he went to work to get the i-ron clads at once in-to deep wa-ter. The lar-gest one—the EAST-PORT—set out first to-ward Al-ex-an-dri-a, but when not more than two miles on her way struck a tor-pe-do, and knocked a large hole in her bot-tom. She was soon a-ground, and Por-ter went with all speed to Al-ex-an-dri-a to get the two steam-ers with steam pumps that he had left there.

At the end of three hours the EAST-PORT was a-float and on her way down the stream in tow of the two steam-ers that pumped her out at the same time. She was a great "ram" that had been built to take part in the fight with a reb-el war-ship of the same sort, and was quite un-fit for use on such a bat-tle field as the Red Riv-er.

THE EAST-PORT TOWED.

They had more or less trou-ble with the big ship for some time. "She would sink," says Por-ter, "and we would pump her out, and get her a-float a-gain; but at last she stuck hard and fast in a bed of logs, and we blew her up with 50 bar-rels of pow-der.

"The reb-els who were close at hand and on the watch for a chance to get the best of our men, made a rush to board the gun-boats that lay at a bank near by, but met with such a hot fire that they were forced to fall back."

In the mean-time, Banks and his troops had left Al-ex-an-dri-a, and gone in-land to meet the foe where the flo-til-la could be of no use to them.

When the fleet left Grand E-core, 500 slaves came on board and begged hard to be ta-ken to the "land of free-dom." When the E<small>AST-PORT</small> was blown up, the Ad-mi-ral put them on the two pump-boats, as he thought that would be a safe place for them, as the reb-els would be more like-ly to at-tack the "tin-clads," as the light-draft gun-boats were called.

But what we least ex-pect is quite sure to take place. As the ves-sels went a-long at a slow pace Por-ter chanced to see some heads stick out of the bush-es on the bank. He sang out to Gor-ringe, "Give those fel-lows in the bush-es a two sec-ond shell!"

In a mo-ment the shell burst in the midst of those on the bank.

"Give them an-oth-er dose!" said Por-ter, when to his great sur-prise there came on board a show-er of shot and shell that made the C<small>RICK-ET</small> shake from stem to stern. Nine-teen shells burst on the ves-sel, and ere those on board of her could fire an-oth-er gun they found them-selves right in front of the reb-el fort, and as the C<small>RICK-ET</small> turned the point the foe poured ten shots in-to her that raked her fore and aft.

THE PI-LOT.

The pi-lot had his head cut

o-pen by a piece of a shell, and still kept at his post.

"I am all right," he said to the Ad-mi-ral. "I won't give up the wheel."

Gor-ringe was quite as cool, and rang the bell for the en-gine to go a-head.

This is the same Lieu-ten-ant Gor-ringe who with great toil, much skill and great risk, brought from Al-ex-an-dria, in E-gypt, the ob-e-lisk which was built near-ly 2,000 years be-fore Christ, and which now stands in Cen-tral Park.

In front of the wheel house lay a heap of dead men— those who had manned the how-itz-ers on the main deck. A shell had struck the gun, which burst and killed all the crew. The worst sight of all was on what is called the fight-ing deck. Here the killed and wound-ed lay all a-round, and but three poor slaves left to man the guns.

"Fire the guns off!" said Por-ter. "Don't let them think we are hurt." The three black men load-ed and fired one of the guns; and there was no one left to fire the next one.

The Ad-mi-ral found the en-gin-eer dead at his post with his hand on the throt-tle valve. As he writhed in his pain, he had turned off the steam and caused the

THE NE-GROES FI-RING THE GUNS.

ves-sel to stop. She was soon sent a-head, and in a short time went round the point and out of range of the earth-works.

The reb-els fired on and sunk the pump-boats, and showed no mer-cy to the poor slaves who swam the riv-er or clung to the wreck. Then they poured their fire on the "tin-clad," JU-LI-ET, raked her fore and aft, cut her stove-pipe in two, and killed and wound-ed many of her crew. She was swept right un-der the bluff where the fort was placed, but as the bluff was 60 feet high, their guns could not reach her, and she had a chance to mend her stove-pipe, and slip off to join her com-rades. The rest of the fleet ran past the fort at night, and had a rough time, but did not fare quite so ill as the CRICK-ET and the JU-LI-ET.

When Por-ter reached Al-ex-an-dri-a he found the fleet high and dry a-bove the Falls; ten gun-boats and two tugs caught in a trap from which there was no way to get out. There seemed naught to do but to wait for a rise.

But as good luck would have it there was a man in Banks' ar-my, who came from the North-west and knew how to build dams. As the reb-els drove our men back, and while the troops were at Grand E-core, this man, Lieu-ten-ant Col-o-nel Bai-ley, had heard of the scant wa-ter at the Falls, and thought he might build a dam there on a large scale that would be of great use. He told his plan to a few friends, all of whom did not think well of it. It came to the ears of the reb-els who made great sport of it, and "How a-bout that dam?" be-came quite a by-word a-mong them. But Bai-ley had great faith, and at last Gen-er-al Banks told him to pick his men and go to work.

A-mong the troops were two or three reg-i-ments from Maine, who had been wood-men and lum-ber-men from their youth. These at once went to work with might and main, and with trained skill, on the trees on the north shore of the Red Riv-er. Oth-ers were found who could lend a hand, and on the 1st of May, 1863, 3,000 men were at work on the dam. At the point where it was to be built the riv-er is 758 feet wide, and the chan-nel was at that time quite strong. The Falls are a mile long, and though the rocks were for the most part bare, the wa-ter—what there was of it—rushed down a-round and o-ver them at a swift rate of speed.

You will see by this that it was no light task to dam up this stream, and make her back wa-ter so that the gun-boats could be set free, and make their way to-ward the Mis-sis-sip-pi.

BUILD-ING THE DAM.

On the north bank a "tree dam" was built of large trees cross-tied with great logs; on this was thrown brush-wood, brick and stone, which the weight of the wa-ter held in place. On the south bank, where there were more rocks than trees, great cribs were pushed out, filled with stones and bricks.

The stones were brought down the riv-er on flat-boats, and the bricks came from hou-ses that were torn down, and from which the reb-els had fled some time be-fore.

A mile off was a large sug-ar house; this was torn down, and the whole of it—bricks, beams, i-ron work, and e-ven the ket-tles —went in-to the dam to help keep it in place. The men kept at work day and night, some up to their waists in wa-ter, some up to their necks, and all full of good cheer and good will.

TEAR-ING DOWN THE SUG-AR HOUSE

This great work was done in eight days, and by its means the wa-ter was raised in the rap-ids to a height of sev-en feet, and on the 12th of May the whole fleet went down the Falls, with the loss of but one man who was swept from the deck of a tug.

For the help that Lieu-ten-ant Bai-ley gave to the na-vy in their hour of need, he was raised to the rank

BUILD-ING THE DAM.

of brig-a-dier gen-er-al, and Con-gress sent him a vote of thanks. No hold was gained in Tex-as by the ar-my or na-vy, and as the war drif-ted a-way from the Mis-sis-sip-pi val-ley, the Squad-ron was not called up-on to fight a-ny great bat-tles. But gun-boats kept on the watch, and like an armed po-lice, went here and there, where-ev-er there was need, to keep the reb-els at bay; and the trans-ports were made use of to bear troops from place to place.

Ad-mi-ral Por-ter tells a strange sto-ry of one of his sail-ors, a man named Self-ridge, who must have been fond of the sea. He was first sunk in the CUM-BER-LAND, in Hamp-ton Roads, by the reb-el ram MER-RI-MAC; then he joined the Mis-sis-sip-pi Squad-ron and was blown up by a tor-pe-do. Por-ter sent him on board the CON-ES-TO-GA, and that ves-sel was run down by a U-ni-on ram and went to the bot-tom. The Ad-mi-ral then placed him on board the NE-O-SHO in hopes to change his luck, and af-ter the fleet came down the Red

IX.—RED RIV-ER EX-PE-DI-TION FLEET PASS-ING THROUGH THE DAM.

Riv-er, Self-ridge was sent up the Mis-sis-sip-pi. In a few days Por-ter went the same way, and found the NE-O-SHO high and dry on a sand-bank!

THE NE-O-SHO HIGH AND DRY.

Self-ridge told his com-mand-er that the reb-els were try-ing to pass some cat-tle o-ver the riv-er, and he made up his mind to stop them.

There was no oth-er road, so they had to turn back, and as the riv-er fell fast the boat was soon stuck fast in the sand.

Por-ter told Self-ridge to pack his trunk and come with him. The ves-sel was in a good place, and com-mand-ed the road, so that no one could get at her to board her, and she was left in charge of the first lieu-ten-ant. Self-ridge was placed in com-mand of the VIN-DI-CA-TOR, a ram of great pow-er, and from that time things went more smooth-ly with him.

He won fame by all of his mis-haps, and proved that he was made of the right kind of stuff. Be-ing a he-ro him-self, one who had been in all the dan-gers of the deep, he was fit to lead and to train oth-ers, and to show how brave a man could be.

CHAPTER X.

BE-FORE MO-BILE.

In the year 1864 the Pres-i-dent made up his mind to seal up the port of Mo-bile, so that no more Brit-ish block-ade run-ners could get in. It was in the month of Jan-u-a-ry, in the midst of a fierce snow-storm, that Far-ra-gut ran up his flag on the Hart-ford and set out for the Gulf of Mex-i-co. He found that great chan-ges had ta-ken place, and but few of his old of-fi-cers were in the Squad-ron.

The reb-els had a large force of gun-boats and i-ron clads in the bay—the ram Ten-nes-see a-mong them—and Far-ra-gut felt that it would be un-wise for him to take in his wood-en ves-sels. The reb-el forts were strong, and it would be no light task to break the block-ade of Mo-bile.

But Far-ra-gut said if he had two i-ron clads he would

soon put an end to this state of things, and he was in haste to "pitch in," as each week of de-lay made it more of a task.

The let-ters he wrote home show what kind of a man he was, and make one feel glad that such a wise, brave, and good man was at the helm.

In the spring of the year, he writes to his son from New Or-le-ans what he thinks of block-a-ding. "But we must take the world as it comes," he says. "This is a state of civ-il war, and God has dealt well with us thus far. When I have done my work, I hope to spend the rest of my days in peace and qui-et in my home on the banks of the Hud-son. It is for man to plan, and God to rule, and I bow to His will, but hope He will grant my pray-er. I ex-pect-ed from the be-gin-ning to fight to the end of this war, or to my end, and I am still read-y and wil-ling to do so if my health will per-mit. This is a day to try men's hearts. It is blow-ing a per-fect gale. The wind howls, the rain pours in tor-rents, and there are quick flash-es of light-ning, and loud peals of thun-der, and all this fills the mind with gloom; yet how thank-ful I feel for the bless-ings I en-joy in be-ing in port, in-stead of out at sea."

On the 24th of A-pril 1864, he writes to his son that

two years a-go he passed Forts Jack-son and St. Phil-ip, and felt as if the fate of the land he loved, and his own life and fu-ture fame, were on the wheel of for-tune to be turned by the fin-ger of the All-Wise. " It was on-ly left to do or die. God was my lead-er, and we passed through a fi-e-ry fur-nace, where none but He could have car-ried us."

Then he wrote what took place on the Red Riv-er at this time, and said, "We dai-ly ex-pect to hear of a bat-tle, but how it will end, God on-ly knows.

" I tell you these things, my boy, that you may learn as you go a-long in life. At a-ny rate, when you get a com-mand, don't put your bag-gage in the way so that you can-not get your troops or guns out ex-cept by stam-pe-ding." A stam-pede is a wild flight that is caused by fright.

In Ju-ly he heard of the fight be-tween the KEAR-SARGE and the AL-A-BA-MA, and says, " I would soon-er have fought that fight than a-ny ev-er fought on the o-ce-an. On-ly think! it was fought like a tour-na-ment in full view of thou-sands of French and En-glish, all of whom thought we would be whipped. Peo-ple came from Par-is to see the fight. The tri-umph of the KEAR-SARGE was grand."

In this same month he wrote of a fight his gun-boats had had with a block-ade run-ner that tried to force her way by them, and spoke thus in praise of his men:
"I have nev-er seen a crew come up like ours. They are a-head of the old set in small arms, and ful-ly e-qual to them at the great guns. They came here a lot of boys and young men, and have now grown stout, and knock the nine inch guns a-bout like 24-pound-ers."

The 4th of Au-gust was fixed as the day for the at-tack on Mo-bile, and Far-ra-gut wrote thus to his wife from on board the flag-ship HART-FORD: "I am go-ing in-to Mo-bile Bay in the morn-ing, if God is my lead-er, as I hope He is, and in Him I place my trust. If He thinks it is the prop-er place for me to die, I am read-y to sub-mit to His will in that as in all oth-er things."

A man who felt like this could not but be calm in the midst of dan-ger, and would have no fear in the face of death.

The i-ron clad TE-CUM-SEH did not come up in time for Far-ra-gut to move on the 4th, but ere day-light of the 5th it hove in sight, and all through the fleet were heard the boat-swains' pipes and calls of "all hands" and "up all ham-mocks."

At four o'clock the wood-en ships were lashed in

SHIPS LASH-ED IN PAIRS.

pairs, and at five the Ad-mi-ral said to the Fleet-Cap-tain, in com-mand of the HART-FORD, "Well, Dray-ton, we might as well get un-der way."

The BROOK-LYN led the fleet, as she had four chase guns, and hooks and chains with which to pick up tor-pe-does. Gun-boats were placed south and east of Fort Mor-gan, to keep up a flank fire on that strong-hold.

By half-past six o'clock the TE-CUM-SEH's guns were heard, to which Fort Mor-gan soon made re-ply. Far-ra-gut gave the sign for "close or-der," and each ves-sel was brought up to with-in a few yards of the one a-head, and the U-ni-on fleet were raked fore and aft by the fire from reb-el forts and gun-boats, be-fore they could bring their broad-sides to bear on the foe.

Cap-tain Dray-ton stood on the poop-deck of the HART-FORD, from whence he gave or-ders to his men. The Ad-mi-ral had climbed up in the rig-ging, on the right side, where he could see all a-bout him, and at the same time speak with Com-mand-er Jou-ett, who stood

X.—PASSING THE FORTS AT MO-BILE BAY.

on the wheel-house of the MET-A-COM-ET, which was lashed a-long-side. Free-man, his trus-ty pi-lot, stood a-bove him in the top.

As the smoke grew thick and shut out his view, the Ad-mi-ral rose step by step un-til he found him-self in what is called the fut-tock shrouds. Dray-ton caught sight of him and fear-ing that a slight shock might throw him in-to the sea, he told Knowles, one of his men, to take up a line and make the Ad-mi-ral more safe.

Knowles went up with a piece of lead-line, and made it fast to one of the for-ward shrouds, and then took it round the Ad-mi-ral to the af-ter shroud, and made it fast there.

The Ad-mi-ral said, "Nev-er mind, I am all right;" but Knowles went a-head and o-bey-ed or-ders, and Far-ra-gut stayed there till the fleet passed in-to the bay.

MAK-ING THE AD-MI-RAL FAST.

When the ram made her at-tack Far-ra-gut made his way to the deck, and when the HART-FORD set out to ram the TEN-NES-SEE he climbed up in-to the *port miz-zen rig-ging* and was made fast there by one of his of-fi-cers. His men showed their love for him by their watch-ful care, and in the hour of dan-ger their first thought was of him who thought not of him-self.

The or-der was to move at slow speed, to get close to the fort, and keep up a fire of shell, shrap-nel, and grape-shot. As the fleet came with-in range the reb-el gun-boats o-pen-ed fire on the HART-FORD, and for 20 min-utes the crash-ing of tim-bers, and the cries of the wound-ed were sounds that sent a thrill of pain through the ill-fated flag-ship.

SINK-ING OF THE TE-CUM-SEH.

Soon the TE-CUM-SEH was well up with the fort, and a-bout to pass the reb-el ram TEN-NES-SEE, when all at once she gave a lurch, and went down with all on board. It was at first thought that the TEN-NES-SEE had sunk, and cheer af-ter cheer went up from the HART-FORD and the rest of the U-ni-on fleet. But Far-ra-gut, from his high perch, saw the true state of things.

Then the BROOK-LYN, which was just a-head of the HART-FORD, be-gan to back, the ves-sels in the rear pressed on those in the van, and there was great con-fu-sion. All this time the reb-els had things their own way, as not a gun was fired from our ships.

A voice shouts through a trum-pet from the flag-ship to the BROOK-LYN, and asks what's the mat-ter.

"Tor-pe-does!" is the shout that comes back.

With an oath Far-ra-gut called out "Four bells! Dray-ton, go a-head! Jou-ett, full speed!" and the HART-FORD steamed past the BROOK-LYN, and took the lead and kept it. It took some time for the rest of the fleet to get back in-to line a-gain, and when they were once more in bat-tle ar-ray, the flag-ship was a mile a-head of them.

Frank-lin Bu-chan-an—who was flag-of-fi-cer on board the MER-RI-MAC—was now in com-mand of the reb-el ram, TEN-NES-SEE. As soon as he caught sight of Far-ra-gut's blue flag, he made a dash to ram the HART-FORD, but failed to do so, and then turned on the BROOK-LYN which by this time was close in her wake. The ram was run a-head as if to butt the U-ni-on ship, which at

THE TEN-NES-SEE AND HART-FORD.

once made plans to sheer off, and then the TEN-NES-SEE turned and poured out a broad-side that made great holes through and through her, and did much harm. This trick was played on each one in turn, while the shots from the U-ni-on fleet struck, and failed to harm, the TEN-NES-SEE's coat of mail, and the reb-el ram went back to her post un-der the guns of Fort Mor-gan.

As soon as Far-ra-gut was clear of the forts, he gave the sig-nal, "Gun-boats, chase the gun-boats of the foe!"

Jou-ett's "Ay, ay, sir!" rang out prompt and clear,

THE TEN-NES-SEE UN-DER THE GUNS OF FORT MOR-GAN.

and he at once set his axe-men to work to cut the MET-A-COM-ET loose from the HART-FORD, and went off with speed to en-gage the MOR-GAN. A thick squall of rain came up and put an end to the fi-ring.

In the mean-time the MET-A-COM-ET, PORT ROY-AL, KEN-NE-BEC and I-TAS-CA gave chase to the SEL-MA, and the MET-A-COM-ET caught her three or four miles up the bay. The MOR-GAN ran a-ground on a spit of land which runs out of Na-vy Cove, but got off a-gain and made her way to Fort Mor-gan, and the same night beat a re-treat to Mo-bile, and was fired on by sev-er-al of our gun-boats.

The fleet came to anch-or three miles up the bay, and the TEN-NES-SEE at once steamed out to-ward the flag-

CHA-SING THE REB-EL GUN-BOATS.

ship. Far-ra-gut's plan was to at-tack the big ram, as soon as it was so dark that the com-mand-er of the fort could not tell friend from foe, but the TEN-NES-SEE had got a-head of him. So he had to make the best of it, and signed to the whole fleet to at-tack the ram with their guns, and with bows on at full speed.

The MON-ON-GA-HE-LA was the first to dash at the ram, which put her helm a-port so that the gun-boat gave her a side-long stroke. Then the ram fired two shots at her foe, and pierced her through and through, while the shot from the MON-ON-GA-HE-LA rolled down its slo-ping sides, and did no harm.

The CHICK-A-SAW then came up, and was re-ceived in much the same way.

The next ves-sel to bear down on her was the LACK-A-WAN-NA, which stove her own bows in by the force of the blow. The TEN-NES-SEE had a slight shock, but soon right-ed her-self and moved on to-ward the HART-FORD, which came out to meet the ram, struck her a fear-ful blow, and poured a broad-side in-to her. Still the mon-ster kept on its way, and gave no signs that it was hurt.

In the mean-time the Mon-i-tors MAN-HAT-TAN, WIN-NE-BA-GO, and CHICK-A-SAW beat the ram with their heav-y shot, un-til her steer-ing gear and smoke-stack were shot a-way, her port shut-ters jammed, and one 15-inch shot had gone through her thick ar-mor!

Her ad-mi-ral is wound-ed, the white-flag is shown, the TEN-NES-SEE sur-rend-ers, "i-ron, yields to oak," and Far-ra-gut is the he-ro of the hour.

The reb-el ram had the best chance for suc-cess as foes were all a-round her, and she could fire from all sides with no fear that she might hit a friend. But this was not the case with the U-ni-on fleet, where the ves-sels had to take great care that they did not fire in-to or strike a-gainst each oth-er. Such an ac-ci-dent did take place: for as the flag-ship was a-bout to at-tack the TEN-NES-SEE she was run in-to by the LACK-A-WAN-NA, and cut down quite near the wa-ter's edge.

At this time the Ad-mi-ral stood aft on the poop-deck. He jumped out-side at once to see how much the HART-FORD was hurt, and at once the cry went round "Get the Ad-mi-ral out of the ship!" The Ad-mi-ral saw that she would still float, and gave or-ders to Dray-ton to drive a-head with all speed and strike the TEN-NES-SEE a-gain. But be-fore the HART-FORD came up the reb-el ram showed the white flag, and the great na-val fight was at an end.

THE WOUND-ED.

The U-ni-on fleet lost 335 men, while the reb-els had but ten killed and 16 wound-ed, and these were on board the TEN-NES-SEE and the SEL-MA. The loss in the forts could not, of course, be known.

Far-ra-gut came on deck just as the poor fel-lows were be-ing laid out, side by side, on the quar-ter deck, and the sight brought tears to his eyes, and he wept like a child.

His vic-to-ry gave great joy to the North, and hosts of let-ters came to Far-ra-gut from friends far and near, full of praise for the brave fight he had fought, and the tri-umph he had won.

THE SUR REN-DER OF THE TEN-NES-SEE

Gen-er-al But-ler wrote, "It is all said in one word: *It was like you.* When I read that 17 of your ves-sels had passed Fort Mor-gan, I called out 'Three cheers for Far-ra-gut!' They were giv-en with a will, and brought in my staff of-fi-cers, who thought their Gen-er-al had gone cra-zy, per-haps from sun-stroke, where-as it was on-ly a stroke of good luck, of high da-ring and no-ble aim, quite as brill-i-ant as a-ny-thing the sun could do.

"Those cheers are not done ring-ing yet; but ev-er-y hill is re-sound-ing with them as they are caught up from ham-let to ham-let, and cit-y to cit-y, of a grate-ful na-tion."

The pa-pers spread the fame of Far-ra-gut far and wide, but he was not a vain man, and was not puffed up by it.

He wrote home, "All I want is to be let a-lone, and to live in peace with my fam-i-ly if I sur-vive this war."

Some of his friends want-ed to run him for Pres-i-dent, but Far-ra-gut said it was his wish to re-main an Ad-mi-ral.

In No-vem-ber, 1864, Far-ra-gut had or-ders to re-turn to the North, and a sa-lute was fired in his hon-or as the flag-ship came in-to the port of New York. He was met by a crowd of the best men of the cit-y, all ea-ger to see and to shake hands with the "He-ro of the Mis-sis-sip-pi," and to thank him for what he had done for the land they loved.

In a speech that Far-ra-gut made, he said that he had

XI.—THE HARTFORD RAMMING THE TENNESSEE.

served his coun-try since he was eight years of age, and that his fa-ther be-fore him had been just as faith-ful. He was glad of his suc-cess, and felt that much praise was due to those of-fi-cers who served with him He gave thanks al-so for the great hon-or that had been paid him; for he now held the high-est rank in the A-mer-i-can Na-vy.

In Jan-u-a-ry, 1865, Far-ra-gut and his wife made a vis-it to their old home at Has-tings-on-the Hud-son, and here they met with a grand dis-play. The streets were spanned with arch-es, on which were the words "New Or-le-ans"—" Mo-bile"—"St. Phil-ip"—"Jack-son"—" Gaines" and " Mor-gan"—in ev-er-green let-ters.

When Rich-mond fell, Far-ra-gut made haste to Wash-ing-ton, and went at once to the Cap-i-tol. One who took note of all that took place here, wrote some-thing in this style: "Through the o-pen door came a smooth-faced man with a keen eye, and a firm, quick step. He wore a plain blue blouse, with three stars on the col-lar. It was the old he-ro who o-pened the way to New Or-le-ans, and who fought the bat-tle of the Mo-bile forts from the mast-head of his ves-sel—Ad-mi-ral Far-ra-gut."

He came to learn the la-test news, and what Grant had done; and when he was told, he gave a great sigh of re-lief, and said, "Thank God, it is a-bout o-ver!" for it was well known that if Lee fell, the South must fall with him.

In the year 1867, Ad-mi-ral Far-ra-gut was placed in com-mand of the Eu-ro-pe-an Squad-ron, and set sail from New York, in the flag-ship FRANK-LIN, on the 28th of June. His wife went with him, and they reached Cher-bourg, France, on the 14th of July.

Some months were spent in crui-sing a-bout the Med-i-ter-ra-ne-an, and in vis-it-ing the chief pla-ces in Eu-rope, and great hon-ors were paid our he-ro where-ev-er he went.

The Prince of Wales came to see him in his roy-al yacht VIC-TO-RI-A and AL-BERT, and as he came on board the FRANK-LIN, he was re-ceived with all the hon-ors due to his rank.

A sa-lute of 21 guns was fired, the Brit-ish flag float-ed from the main-mast, and the band played "God save the Queen."

In a few days the Ad-mi-ral was in-vi-ted to Os-borne House, where the Queen of En-gland lives, and was pre-sent-ed to her Maj-es-ty, who re-ceived him in a kind way, and with no pomp or pa-rade.

In the sum-mer of 1869, the Ad-mi-ral and his wife

vis-it-ed the Pa-cif-ic Coast, where he met with old friends who gave him a warm wel-come, and paid him high hon-ors.

In Far-ra-gut Park, Wash-ing-ton, and in Cen-tral Park, New York, were placed large bronze stat-ues of Ad-mi-ral Far-ra-gut, and in such ways the peo-ple sought to show their love for the brave com-mand-er.

He was a man of deep feel-ing, and his trust in God gave him strength when he felt how vain was the help of man. It is said that when the TE-CUM-SEH went down and the BROOK-LYN stopped, he was at a loss to know just what it was best to do. He lift-ed his heart to God, and asked "Shall I go on?" and it seemed to him as if he heard a voice com-mand him to "Go on!" and he went on, and won the fight.

A three years' war, in which the Ad-mi-ral took part in 11 bat-tles, was a great strain up-on a man of his age, and his health soon be-gan to fail.

In the sum-mer of 1870, he was placed in com-mand of the dis-patch steam-er TAL-LA-POO-SA, and as it drew near the na-vy yard at Ports-mouth, New Hamp-shire, the Ad-mi-ral seemed to feel that his end was near. At the sound of the sa-lute that was fired to do him hon-or, he rose from his sick bed, dressed him-self in his full u-ni-form and went on deck. He looked up with a sad smile at his blue flag that float-ed from the mast-head, and said "It would be well if I died *now*, in har-ness."

One day la-ter, he was heard to say, as he stepped from the sloop-of-war DALE, that was then at the wharf, "That is the last time I shall ev-er tread the deck of a man-of-war." This proved true; and on the 14th of Au-gust, 1870, at the age of 69, the good old Ad-mi-ral passed a-way from earth.

His aim in life had been to do his du-ty wher-ev-er he was placed. "No man," he said, "can tell what he will do in a cer-tain place till he finds him-self in it." Suc-cess did not come to him all at once, but he won it step by step, by hard work, by strong faith in him-self, and a firm trust in God. He did not send his men where he would not go him-self, but *took the lead* and fought the foe at short range.

Fit to rank with En-gland's great na-val com-mand-er, Lord Ho-ra-tio Nel-son, the "He-ro of Traf-al-gar," is A-mer-i-ca's High Ad-mi-ral, Da-vid Glas-gow Far-ra-gut—"Old heart of oak!"

CHAPTER XI.

A YOUNG HE-RO.

A YOUNG man in the ar-my has more chance to do great deeds, than one in the na-vy, who has to o-bey or-ders and keep with-in a small space. Mere boys left their homes and went in-to bat-tle with all the zeal of full-grown men, and risked their lives to save the hon-or of the dear old flag they had been taught to re-spect and love.

Some of these won high praise for the part they took in the great war, and not a few of them rose to high rank.

No young man in the na-vy was quite so bold as Lieu-ten-ant Wil-li-am B. Cush-ing, of whose deeds I will tell you.

The coast of North Car-o-li-na is so bro-ken up with bays, sounds, and in-lets, that it was hard work for the Squad-ron to keep up the block-ade there. Though they tried their best to lock up the port of Wil-ming-ton, they could not keep out the block-ade run-ners, 65 of which were seized dur-ing the war.

The town of Wil-ming-ton is on Cape Fear Riv-er

20 miles from its mouth. There were two ways of reaching Cape Fear Riv-er: one from the east-ward, through New In-let; and one from the south, at the riv-er's mouth. These are six miles a-part, and be-tween them lies Smith Isl-and, a long strip of sand and shoal. A-long the line of Cape Fear, the Fry-ing Pan Shoals stretch themselves out for ten miles, so that the dis-tance by wa-ter be-tween the two in-lets is not much less than 40 miles.

Strong works were on each of these chan-nels, and each one had to have a block-a-ding force.

The block-ade run-ners would start out from Smith ville, a small town on the Cape Fear Riv-er, and drop down to Wil-ming-ton, where they would watch their chance, and make their choice be-tween New In-let and the main chan-nel.

Fort Fish-er was on Fed-er-al Point, at the north of New In-let; and Fort Cas-well was at the mouth of the riv-er. A sharp look-out was kept from these forts, and if a block-a-der came too near a shell would soon warn him of the fact, and he would make haste to get out of range. Block-ade run-ners would wait out-side un-til it was dark, then dash at full speed through the fleet, and get un-der the guns of the fort, where they would be safe. This is why it was so hard to close the port of

Wil-ming-ton, e-ven though 50 steam-ers were on guard, some of them the fast-est in our Na-vy.

On the night of Feb-ru-a-ry 28, 1864, Cush-ing, who was in com-mand of the MON-TI-CEL-LO, fit-ted out two boats, took with him En-sign Jones, Mas-ter's mate How-arth, and twen-ty men, and went past the fort and up the riv-er to Smith-ville. His aim was to land at the town, seize the of-fi-cer in com-mand, and board the ves-sels he might find in the har-bor. It was a great risk to run for so small a prize, for Smith-ville was not much of a place, and the cap-ture of twelve of-fi-cers in com-mand there, would not pay for the loss of one Cush-ing.

LIEU-TEN-ANT CUSH-ING ON HIS WAY TO SMITH-VILLE.

But he went to work with great cool-ness and bold-ness, and as if there was no such word as fail, and land-ed his boats in front of the ho-tel at Smith-ville. He hid his men un-der the bank, and went off a-lone to seize some slaves from whom he learned what he wished to know. Then he came back to the shore, and ta-king with him the two of-fi-cers and a sea-man, walked to Gen-er-al Her-bert's head-quar-ters, right in front of the bar-racks, where were 1,000 reb-els, who with ease might have caught the rash young Yan-kees.

Gen-er-al Her-bert had gone to Wil-ming-ton, so Cush-ing went in the house and seized an of-fi-cer not so high in rank. The Ad-ju-tant Gen-er-al ran in great haste to the woods, and did not think to call out the troops, so Cush-ing took his pris-on-er to the boat, and passed with-in a few yards of the sen-try on the wharf.

In a short time af-ter he had set sail from Smith-ville, a sig-nal was made to Fort Cas-well that boats were in the har-bor, but Cush-ing had passed the fort be-fore its guns could o-pen fire.

CUSH-ING CAP-TURES THE AD-JU-TANT GEN-ER-AL

The next bold deed that Cush-ing did took place in June of the same year. On the night of the 23rd he left the MON-TI-CEL-LO, and went on board one of the small boats—called a cut-ter—with Jones and How-arth and 15 sea-men. The moon came out when they were a-bout 15 miles from the mouth of the riv-er, so that they were seen by the sen-tries on the bank. Cush-ing made a feint of go-ing back, but as soon as he reached the shore where the shad-ows were thick, he changed his course and kept on up the stream to-ward Wil-ming-ton. To-ward morn-ing, when with-in sev-en miles of Wil-ming-ton, he came to land and hid the boat in a swamp.

HI-DING THE CREW.

The crew kept out of sight all day, and watched the riv-er, and at night, as they were read-y to move, they seized two boat loads of men who had been off to catch fish, and forced them to serve as guides. The rest of that night Cush-ing spent in no-ting how the reb-els had blocked the riv-er be-low the town. At day-break he moved up one of the creeks where he found a road, and leav-ing a few men in the boat he land-ed, and walked on un-til he came to the main road be-tween Wil-ming-ton and Fort Fish-er. Here he lay in wait, and soon there came a-long a man on horse-back with the mail from the fort. Cush-ing seized the man, the horse and the mail-bag, and in two hours a-long came a horse-man from the town. This man, how-ev-er, caught sight of a blue-coat and made off with all speed. Cush-ing went af-ter him on the horse he had seized, but the man had a good start and a bet-ter steed, and so made his es-cape.

CHA-SING THE REB-EL HORSE-MAN.

Cush-ing had been a-way from the boat for some hours, and his men had had noth-ing to eat, so he at once set to work to get them some food. He learned from pris-on-ers whom he seized, that a store was to be found two miles off, so he had How-arth put on the mail car-ri-er's coat and hat, mount his horse, and ride to mar-ket.

How-arth, who had a bold air, and was quite at his ease, made free to talk with the folks he met on the road, and gave none of them cause to think that he was a foe in dis-guise. He soon came back with a large sup-ply of food; and af-ter a good meal, the men a-mused them-selves for a while by cut-ting the tel-e-graph wires, and at dark went on board the boat.

On the third night Cush-ing set out to re-turn to the

HOW-ARTH GO-ING TO MAR-KET.

Mon-ti-cel-lo, and on the way down the riv-er he set his pris-on-ers a-drift in boats, with-out oars or sails, that they might not make it known too soon how near he was, and what deeds he had done.

As he reached the mouth of the riv-er the moon came out and he was seen by a guard-boat. As he was a-bout to at-tack her, three oth-ers came out of the dark side of the stream, and at the same in-stant five more came up on the oth-er side. As Cush-ing turned the cut-ter to-ward the on-ly place left o-pen, he found a schoon-er filled with troops a-head of him.

For a mo-ment it seemed as if all was lost, but Cush-ing's pluck did not fail him. He made a dash to-ward the bar on the west, and the reb-els tried to head him off, but lost sight of him for a time; then he watched his chance, gave a quick turn to his boat, and went at full speed to-ward New In-let. The men were as cool as their mas-ter; their oars kept time, and at each pull the boat shot a-head, and ere long was out in the break-

CUSH-ING'S ES-CAPE.

ers where the foe did not dare to fol-low. The cut-ter came back from her three days' cruise in as good or-der as she set out, and the fame of Cush-ing's deed was noised through the land, and he at once took high rank as a "dare dev-il."

In 1864 the reb-el ram AL-BE-MARLE was launched, and sent down the Ro-an-oake Riv-er, to aid in an at-tack on the U-ni-on force at Ply-mouth, which be-gan A-pril 18th. At this time Lieu-ten-ant Flus-ser was in com-mand of the gun-boats MI-AM-I, the SOUTH-FIELD, and two tugs used as pick-et boats. The gun-boats threw shells at the foe du-ring the fight on shore, and in this way drove them back from the forts.

The next day, when word came that the AL-BE-MARLE

was on its way down the riv-er, the two gun-boats were lashed side by side. At mid-night the pick-et boat brought word that the reb-el ram was close at hand. She moved at a slow rate of speed and made straight for the SOUTH-FIELD. Her ports were closed and she did not fire a shot, but she struck the SOUTH-FIELD on the star-board bow and forced her ram in-to the fire-room. As soon as the ram was drawn out the SOUTH-FIELD filled and sank.

THE AL-BE-MARLE AND THE SOUTH-FIELD.

Both ves-sels kept up a sharp fire, but when the shells struck the i-ron sides of the ram they burst and flew all o-ver the deck of the MI-AM-I. Three or four of these bits of shell struck and killed the brave Flus-ser, and wound-ed six oth-ers, but no harm was done to the AL-BE-MARLE.

The ropes gave way that bound the two boats, and the crew of the sink-ing SOUTH-FIELD jumped on board the MI-AM-I, which with-drew from the fight, and, with the two tugs, dropped down to the mouth of the riv-er The AL-BE-MARLE gave chase for a while, and shots flew back and forth, but did no harm. The next day the white flag gave to-ken of the sur-ren-der of Plym-outh.

On the 5th of May, the AL-BE-MARLE came down the riv-er, with a steam-er filled with troops and a trans-port filled with food and coal, to cruise a-bout in the sounds.

The Squad-ron met her ten miles from the mouth of the riv-er, and here a fight took place, and the ram was for a-while be-tween two fires. Al-though not much hurt, her store ves-sel was seized, and she was at last forced to turn back. A plan was made to blow up the ram with tor-pe-does, placed in the riv-er,

PLA-CING TOR-PE-DOES.

XII.—BLOWING UP THE AL-BER-MARLE.

but the men in charge had poor luck, and bare-ly es-
caped with their lives.

Then the War De-part-ment at Wash-ing-ton thought of a scheme by which the reb-el ram could be got rid of, and they chose Cush-ing to car-ry it out. Two steam launch-es, or pick-et boats, were fitted out at New York, and rigged with spar tor-pe-does. Both were to have been used, but as one of them was lost in cross-ing Ches-a-peake Bay, Cush-ing—in no wise cast down by this ill-luck—made haste to do the best that he could with the boat that was left.

It was late in Oc-to-ber when Cush-ing reached Al-be-marle sound, where quite a fleet of boats were on guard. Here he spent a few days, took on more of-fi-cers and sea-men, and then was towed up the sound by the OT-SE-GO.

The reb-el ram lay at the dock at Plym-outh, on the right side of the Ro-an-oake Riv-er, eight miles from its mouth. The shore on both sides was lined with pick-ets, and the reb-els kept a close watch on the wreck of the SOUTH-FIELD. Cush-ing knew all this, but felt no fear.

With him on the launch were Mas-ter's Mates How-arth, Gay, and Wood-man; Pay-mas-ter Swan; two en-gi-neer of-fi-cers, Stee-ver and Stotes-bu-ry; and eight sea-men. Each man had his place on the boat—at the bow, near the wheel, or at the stern—and knew just what he had to do.

The tor-pe-do was placed at the end of a spar, at the star-board bow of the launch, and Cush-ing stood on deck and held the lines that would guide and set it off. The night was dark. Now and then the rain fell in great sheets. The launch crept close by the trees on the right bank, and moved slow-ly up the stream.

LAUNCH, WITH SPAR TOR-PE-DOES.

Cush-ing's plan was, if he could get on shore with-out be-ing seen, to land be-low the ram, board her at the wharf, and bring her down the riv-er.

It seems strange that he should have thought of such a wild scheme; but his aim was to take the reb-els by sur-prise, and if he failed in this, to at-tack with the tor-pe-do.

The launch went by the SOUTH-FIELD, but no guns were fired at her from the guard-boats, that were not on the look-out for such craft. Soon they came to a bend in the stream, an o-pen stretch of wa-ter, like a bay, on which lay the town of Plym-outh.

Now the risk was great, as the lights on the shore sent their bright rays o-ver the wa-ter.

Still the launch kept on, and drew up to-wards the logs that made a sort of fence a-round the AL-BE-MARLE. The bark of a dog roused the watch-man, and the glare of a fire on the bank lit up the launch so that it could not fail to be seen. The time for a sur-prise had gone by. Cush-ing had to change his plan at once, and to work with speed and skill in or-der to save his own life and the lives of those who were with him.

Cush-ing, stand-ing at the bow, cried out with a loud voice "A-head fast!" and the launch made a dash to-ward the reb-el ram, and struck hard a-gainst the logs that shut her in. At the same time the OT-SE-GO was cut loose and sent down the riv-er, to seize the guards that kept watch by the wreck of the SOUTH-FIELD.

The air was full of bul-lets. Some of the men on board the launch were hurt, but Cush-ing did not have time to think of them. His whole mind was on the tor-pe-do, which he let down so that it would strike the i-ron-clad be-low the wa-ter line.

As he drew near he cried out at the top of his voice, "Leave the ram! We are go-ing to blow you up!"

Then he dropped the tor-pe-do with one line, and as he felt it rise and touch the bot-tom of the AL-BE-MARLE, he drew hard on the trig-ger line and burst it. At the same time one of the AL-BE-MARLE's big guns was fired, but though she was with-in a few feet of the ram the launch was un-hurt. But the worst harm came from the tor-pe-do, that threw up a great vol-ume of wa-ter, which fell on the launch and held her fast a-mong the logs.

When Cush-ing saw that he could not get his boat off, he paid no heed to the reb-el cries of "Sur-ren-der! Sur-ren-der!" but called out to his crew "Save your-selves!" took off his coat and his shoes and sprang in-to the riv-er. Some of the men did the same, and but three of these were lost.

SAVE YOUR-SELVES.

Half a mile down the riv-er

Cush-ing came a-cross Mas-ter's Mate Wood-man, and did all he could to aid him, but failed to get him a-shore. He was so weak him-self when he reached the bank that he could not crawl out of the wa-ter, but lay there un-til day-light. The next day he stole in-to the swamp near the fort, and worn out as he was, walked for miles and miles o-ver the soft ground. On the way he met a black man whom he sent to find out all he could a-bout last-night's work. When the word came back that the reb-el ram was sunk, Cush-ing kept on with a light heart till he came to a creek, where he found a skiff in which he made his way the next night to the pick-et boat at the mouth of the riv-er.

ES-CAPE IN A SKIFF.

Those who would not or could not leave the launch, had to sur-ren-der to the foe, and were ta-ken a-shore by a boat from the AL-BE-MARLE. The ram sank at the wharf, and lay there till Plym-outh was re-ta-ken, and the steam-launch had done all that it set out to do.

Cush-ing at this time was but 21 years of age. He

was six feet in height, and quite slen-der, and though at heart a boy, full of fun, fond of rash deeds, as bold as a hawk, and as brave as a li-on, he had the mind of a man to plan great deeds and to take the lead-ing part in them him-self.

He won fame young, and stands at the bow, in front of all the na-val he-roes of the four years' war.

CHAPTER XII.

THE AT-TACK ON FORT FISH-ER.

FORT FISH-ER, as I have told you, was one of the de-fen-ces of Wil-ming-ton, and stood on a bluff at the mouth of Cape Fear Riv-er. It was a strong fort, armed with large guns, from whose great throats poured forth such a stream of shot and shell that no boats would dare come with-in range.

It had 21 guns on the land side, and 17 guns on what is termed the sea face. The par-a-pets were 25 feet thick, and 20 feet in height, al-most their whole length. Then there were 30 bomb-proofs and pla-ces for the sto-ring of pow-der; and be-side these the main mag-a-zine, or

XIII.—BOMBARDMENT OF FORT FISHER.

store-house, where tons and tons of pow-der were kept for use in the great guns.

A long line of ri-fle pits at the rear, and a line of tor-pe-does in front, kept the U-ni-on na-vy and ar-my at bay, and the reb-el flag at high-mast. But this state of things could not last much long-er, and in the sum-mer of 1864, plans were laid to have the ar-my and na-vy u-nite in an at-tack on Fort Fish-er.

Ves-sels of all kinds were sent to Hamp-ton Roads to form a war-fleet, un-der com-mand of Ad-mi-ral Por-ter. Troops were to be sent by Grant, but he could not spare them just at that time, and Por-ter could not move un-til they came. The war-fleet might blow up the fort, and dis-lodge the guns, but troops must be near at hand to drive out the reb-els and take the fort in-to their own hands.

In No-vem-ber, Grant sent 6,000 troops un-der Gen-er-al Weit-zel to aid Ad-mi-ral Por-ter, and on the 14th of De-cem-ber, the war-ves-sels and trans-ports, to the num-ber of 75 or 80, moved out of Hamp-ton Roads and met on the At-lan-tic, 25 miles east of the fort.

The Ad-mi-ral's flag-ship was the MAL-VERN, a wood-en riv-er or bay steam-er.

The plan was to blow up Fort Fish-er with a pow-der

boat, or float-ing mine, which should be brought as near the fort as it could be got, and then set off.

This pow-der boat was fit-ted up with great care, and at great risk. Piles and piles of bags filled with pow-der were brought on board, and each bag had a piece of fuse round it so that it would be sure to go off. In the cab-in was a clock set at the time they wished the fuse to start. There were can-dles that would burn a-while and then burst; and hand gre-nades that would fall and set the boat on fire; and pine knots piled up that were to be lit by the last man that left the ship, and which would be sure to add to the fu-ry of the flame.

EX-PLO-SION OF THE POW-DER BOAT.

Gen-er-al But-ler's trans-ports were at New In-let, but Por-ter thought they would be on the ground in time to seize the fort, so on Christ-mas eve he set off the mine. But all of the pow-der did not go off, and the well-planned scheme came to naught.

XIV.—ASSAULT ON THE LAND SIDE OF FORT FISHER.

The noise woke up the reb-els in the fort, and for some hours there was a sharp fire of shot and shell from the earth-works and the ships' guns.

The next day, Christ-mas, the ar-my and na-vy joined in the at-tack, but with no great suc-cess. Por-ter fired 18,000 shots and shells, while but 700 were sent from the fort, which led the Ad-mi-ral to think that the force there was weak. So he brought the MAL-VERN near Gen-er-al But-ler's ship, and shout-ed through his trum-pet, "Gen-er-al, there is not a reb-el with-in five miles of the fort. You have noth-ing to do but to march in and take it."

This was mere guess work on the part of Ad-mi-ral Por-ter. The truth was, that there were at least 900 men in the fort, and but one of the 20 guns on the land face had been harmed by the fire from the fleet.

But-ler at once set out to land his troops, but the wind rose and drove the surf so high that they had to be called back, and the at-tack ceased for a time.

Ad-mi-ral Por-ter, who was a quick, proud man, and apt to speak out his mind, wrote thus to Gen-er-al Grant: "Send me the same sol-diers with an-oth-er Gen-er-al, and we will have the fort." Grant at once gave heed to this re-quest, and on the 6th of Jan-u-a-ry,

1865, 8,000 troops, in com-mand of Gen-er-al A. H. Ter-ry, left Hamp-ton Roads, and joined the war-fleet off Beau-fort, North Car-o-li-na.

On the 12th, they all went down the coast, and the same night were in front of Fort Fish-er.

Fierce gales blew, and high seas tossed the boats a-bout, but they rode them safe-ly, and were in good or-der to take part in the fight. They sailed in three lines.

ON THE WAY TO FORT FISH-ER—SEC-OND AT-TACK.

At day-light the three lines came to anch-or at Half Moon bat-ter-y, four miles north of Fort Fish-er, and in a short time boats were sent to the trans-ports and the troops were borne to land.

The first line of ves-sels shelled the woods back of the fort, and hun-dreds of cat-tle that had been brought there to feed the troops in the fort, ran down to the

LAND-ING TROOPS.

beach, and gave them-selves up to our men who were glad of such a sup-ply of fresh beef.

At 3 o'clock in the af-ter-noon all the troops had land-ed, and the whole fleet moved up near the fort. All the night be-fore the i-ron clads had pound-ed at the fort, and now the ves-sels set in to at-tack the land side.

The scene was now a grand one. Shells hissed through the air, blazed and flashed, and then burst with a fear-ful noise. At times great clouds of smoke and sand hid the fort from sight, and were touched here and there with glints of gold from the set-ting sun. By six o'clock it was too dark to see how to fire, so the wood-en ves-sels were drawn off and ta-ken out to sea, where they dropped anch-ors, while the i-ron clads were left to keep up a slow fire on the works through the night.

Gen-er-al Ter-ry went on board the flag-ship, MAL-VERN, to talk with Ad-mi-ral Por-ter, and to plan the work that was to be done the next day. The troops had thrown up earth-works a-cross the point of land

BUILD-ING BREAST WORKS.

a-bout two miles north of Fort Fish-er, so that there would be no chance for the reb-els to es-cape by land should the fort be taken.

The Ad-mi-ral's or-ders were that 1,600 sail-ors and 400 ma-rines should " board the sea face, while the troops as-sault-ed the land side."

The sea-men were to be armed with sharp cut-lass-es and re-vol-vers. The or-der to com-mand-ers ran thus:

" When the sig-nal is made to man the boats, the men will get in, but not show them-selves. When the sig-nal is made to as-sault, the boats will pull a-round the stern of the mon-i-tors and land right a-breast of them, and board the fort in a sea-man-like way. The ma-rines will form in the rear and cov-er the sail-ors. While the sol-diers are go-ing o-ver the par-a-pets in front, the sail-ors will take the sea-face of Fort Fish-er."

BOATS AD-VAN-CING TO THE AS-SAULT.

"This," as Ad-mi-ral Am-men says, "was more eas-i-ly said than done;" but some plan had to be made, and great men al-ways aim to do great things.

Lieu-ten-ant Com-mand-er Breese led the as-sault, The men were placed in four lines: first the ma-rines, un-der Cap-tain L. L. Daw-son; the rest sail-ors, from the fleet, in charge of Cap-tains Cush-man, Par-ker and Self-ridge.

Work be-gan on the morn-ing of the 15th of Jan-u-a-ry, but it was not un-til three in the af-ter-noon that the sig-nal was giv-en to bom-bard the fort.

SAIL-ORS DASH A-HEAD TO TAKE THE FORT.

All the ves-sels in the fleet blew off steam at the same time with a shriek that must have been heard for miles and miles, and in the midst of the noise both troops and sail-ors dashed a-head to take the fort or die in the at-tempt.

Shells burst o-ver the

XV.—IN-TE-RI-OR OF FORT FISH-ER.

walls of Fort Fish-er, and let the reb-els with-in know that some move was to be made by the U-ni-on force.

The troops on the land side pushed their way forward, and gained and held the west-ern end of the par-a-pet, but the sail-ors and ma-rines had to face such a storm of shells and grape-shot that they could not gain much ground. Twice were they swept back, and a-gain brought up to face the hill that seemed one mass of fire. Brave as the men were, there was small chance for a foot-hold on the sea-front, but some of them did make out to scale the walls and join the ar-my lines.

SEA-FACE OF FORT.

The i-ron clads lent all the aid they could, and the U-ni-on men pressed on from the rear, and by night-fall had won quite a strong hold of parts of the reb-el fort. When it was too dark for them to be seen by the foe, our na-val he-roes, who had been kept on the beach, made their way round to the rear of the fort and joined the troops there, or went with them up to-ward the fort.

Cush-ing, who was wound-ed, brought a band of the sail-ors to the rear, and took charge of a line of breast-works, so that the troops who had been on guard there might join their com-rades in the fort.

The reb-els looked for aid from Gen-er-al Bragg, but he did not ap-pear, and would have had hard work to pass his troops in front of the fire from our gun-boats.

The bat-tle raged hot with-in the fort. Men fired in each oth-er's fa-ces, and fought more like wild beasts than hu-man be-ings. Through all the war there had been no scene like this. It was the last death-strug-gle of the reb-els, and they fought most brave-ly. But the U-ni-on force was too strong for them, and at ten o'clock at night they be-gan to yield. Some of them fled —the white flag gave the sign of sur-ren-der—rock-ets went up from the fleet—and all the reb-el works on the Cape Fear Riv-er knew that Fort Fish-er was in

FIGHT-ING IN THE TRAV-ER-SES.

THE WHITE FLAG.

the hands of the U-ni-on men, and were warned that they must sur-ren-der or scat-ter.

They chose to save them-selves by flight; and so the works that guard-ed Cape Fear Riv-er, with all their great guns and small arms, fell in-to U-ni-on hands, and in a few weeks the stars and stripes waved o-ver Wil-ming-ton, and U-ni-on hearts were filled with joy.

The war was not yet at an end, how-ev-er, for Sher-man had not set out on his march at this time, and Grant was still at Pe-ters-burg. But the at-tack on Fort Fish-er was the last na-val bat-tle that was fought, and it stands out bright on the page of his-to-ry, and adds much to the fame of our na-val he-roes.

Gen-er-al Ter-ry won high rank and much praise for his skill and brav-er-y, and his name will al-ways stand out in bold type, when-ev-er we read of Fort Fish-er, and how it was ta-ken. But words seem weak when we would tell of the deeds of the brave sea-men, who in all bat-tles have to face two great foes. On one side are the guns that send forth a fire whose touch is death; and on the oth-er side is the deep, deep sea, which all too soon may be their grave. So it seems to me that a man or a boy who joins the na-vy has need of strong nerves, a brave heart, a clear head, a firm will, and a soul at peace with God, and then he will be sure to dare great deeds, to do just what needs to be done, and to prove him-self a he-ro where-ev-er he may be. The deck of a ship is no place for a cow-ard, and he who learns to o-bey, and to do his du-ty as a cab-in boy, may rise to take com-mand of a ship, or of a whole fleet, and wear the stars of a Cap-tain or an Ad-mi-ral.

AP-PEN-DIX.

NA-VAL HE-ROES OF THE WAR WITH SPAIN.

THE years that passed be-tween the close of the war with the South and the out-break of that with Spain saw vast chan-ges in the style of war-ships. The great na-tions of Eu-rope had seen the use we had made of i-ron-clads, and knew that the day of the ship built of wood had gone by. They set to work to plan and build ships cov-ered with thick-er and thick-er plates of hard steel, and armed with guns that had more pow-er and that could be fired more rap-id-ly, till the man-of-war grew to be a thing not much like what it was be-fore the fight be-tween the MON-I-TOR and the MER-RI-MAC.

For a long time aft-er peace was re-stored, our gov-ern-ment built no new ships. A great debt had to be paid, and men were so tired of war and its hor-rors that they hoped nev-er to see it a-gain. But a day came when our peo-ple a-woke to the facts that we were too far be-hind other coun-tries in na-val strength, that the old ships which had done such good ser-vice in their time were now out of date, and that, to be safe, we must have some new ones, as strong, as swift, and as well-armed as they could be made.

In 1883 the keels were laid of four fine ships, the AT-LAN-TA, the BOS-TON, the CHI-CA-GO, and the DOL-PHIN, and these, from the first let-ters of their names, were called the A, B, C, D of our new na-vy.

THE AT-LAN-TA.   THE BOS-TON.   THE CHI-CA-GO.   THE DOL-PHIN.

The work of build-ing new ships went on through the years that fol-lowed, till we be-gan to be a-ble to make a fair show of strength on the sea. The best mod-els in for-eign na-vies were stud-ied by our ex-perts, and their own wits were kept hard at work, so that our ships might have all good points, and be fit to cope with the strong-est that might come a-gainst them. We were proud of our grand men-of-war, and no one feared that our na-vy would not be a-ble to give a good ac-count of it-self if called up-on to de-fend the coun-try or its hon-or.

The de-struc-tion of one of these ships was the di-rect cause of the out-break of the war with Spain. A re-bel-lion a-gainst the rule of that pow-er in the isl-and of Cu-ba had be-gun in the year 1895. The Am-er-i-can peo-ple are al-ways apt to side with those who are strug-gling for free-dom, and in this case the feel-ing had grown quite strong with most of them through hear-ing tales, some false, but man-y true, of the cru-el meth-ods Spain was us-ing to put down the reb-els. Spain did not like this, and so there was a great deal of ill feel-ing.

Ear-ly in the year 1898, it had been thought wise to send a U. S. war-ship, the MAINE, to Hav-a-na, the Cap-i-tal of Cu-ba, to pro-tect Am-er-i-cans who had bus-i-ness there. On the night of Feb-ru-a-ry 15th, a-bout 10 o'clock, while most of the crew were a-sleep, a ter-ri-ble ex-plo-sion took place on this ship, by which it was com-plete-ly wrecked, and 266 of the men killed or drowned. The coun-try was hor-ri-fied when the news of this came, and from all lips were heard the questions, Was it an accident, or was it done by design? If the latter, was it done by Spaniards, or by Cubans who wished to anger the Americans against Spain?

To get answers to these questions, President McKinley appointed a Court of Inquiry to seek out the facts. This Court went to Havana, and after hearing much testimony, made a report that the MAINE had been blown up from the outside by a mine or torpedo. The evidence did not warrant the Court in charging the crime on any person or persons, but it was the belief of the greater part of the American people that Spanish officials had had a hand in it. They felt that a government under which such a thing could take place was not fit to rule, and that this country had a right to demand that Spain should grant freedom to Cuba, and leave the island herself.

Spain denied that she had had anything to do with the loss of the MAINE. She offered to leave that question to the arbitration of other nations, but she positively refused to give up Cuba, and the people of the United States had to decide whether or not they would go to war to make her do so. They decided on war, and on April 19th, 1898, Congress passed a resolu-

XVI.—BLOWING UP OF THE MAINE.

tion de-mand-ing that Spain with-draw from Cu-ba, and di-rect-ing the Pres-i-dent, in case she still re-fused, to use the ar-my and na-vy to force her to go.

Ac-tive pre-par-a-tions for war had been go-ing on ev-er since the loss of the MAINE. Our na-vy, in num-ber of ships and in gun-pow-er, was not much, if an-y, strong-er than that of Spain, so all was done that could be done to add to it. There was no time to build—the new style of war-ship is a long time in ma-king—so a-gents were sent a-broad to buy all the ar-mored ships that were for sale. Not man-y could be got. Three cruis-ers were bought in Eng-land, and a tor-pe-do boat in Ger-ma-ny. At home, the gov-ern-ment did once more what it had done at the out-break of the Civ-il War, as has been told in the first chap-ter of this book. It bought a great lot of un-ar-mored ships of all sorts, steam-ers, yachts, tugs, etc, and sup-plied them with guns. These craft formed what was called the aux-il-ia-ry branch of the na-vy. They could scout the sea, help in block-ades, cap-ture Span-ish mer-chant-men, car-ry mes-sa-ges and sup-plies, and in fact do al-most all that a war-ship has to do, ex-cept meet the heav-i-ly armed ships of the foe in fight. And, as things turned out, some of these ships did give bat-tle to ar-mored foes with-out get-ting much harm from them. The lar-gest and best known of the aux-il-ia-ry cruis-ers were four great steam-ers of the Am-er-i-can Line, the ST. PAUL, the ST. LOU-IS, the NEW YORK, and the PAR-IS. The ST. PAUL was as-signed to Cap-tain Sigs-bee, who had been in com-mand of the MAINE when she was blown up. The NEW YORK and the PAR-IS were re-named the HAR-VARD and the YALE.

When the war be-gan, a large fleet, un-der com-mand of Act-ing Rear Ad-mi-ral Samp-son, had gath-ered at

CAP-TURE OF A SPAN-ISH MER-CHANT-MAN.

Key West, our near-est port to Cu-ba. No-tice was served on for-eign na-tions of our in-tent to block-ade Hav-an-a and oth-er Cu-ban ports, and on A-pril 21st, Ad-mi-ral Samp-son set sail with his fleet to en-force the block-ade. On A-pril 23d, the first cap-tures of Span-ish ships were made, two schoon-ers and a steam-er be-ing taken. On A-pril 27th, the first ac-tion of the war took place, the earth-works of Ma-tan-zas, Cu-ba, be-ing bom-bard-ed and si-lenced by the NEW YORK (Ad-mi-ral Samp-son's flag-ship,) the PU-RI-TAN, and the CIN-CIN-NA-TI.

While peo-ple were watch-ing these do-ings on the Cu-ban coast, a sur-prise from the oth-er side of the world was in store for them. The out-break of the war had found sta-tioned at Hong Kong, in Chi-na, an Am-er-i-can squad-ron un-der com-mand of Com-mo-dore George Dew-ey. His flag-ship was the first-class pro-tect-ed cruis-er, O-LYM-PI-A, and his oth-er ships were the cruis-ers RA-LEIGH, BAL-TI-MORE, and BOS-TON, the gun-boats CON-CORD, and PE-TREL, and the dis-patch boat, MC CUL-LOCH. Sev-en hun-dred miles a-way, at Man-il-a, the cap-i-tal of the Phil-ip-pines, a group of isl-ands owned by Spain, was a Span-ish fleet, great-er in num-ber than Com-mo-dore Dew-ey's, but com-posed of less mod-ern

THE PU-RI-TAN, NEW YORK, AND CIN-CIN-NA-TI BOM-BARD-ING MA-TAN-ZAS.

ships. Com-mo-dore Dew-ey re-ceived or-ders by ca-ble from Wash-ing-ton to "find the Span-ish fleet, and cap-ture and des-troy it," and nev-er were or-ders more com-plete-ly car-ried out.

On A-pril 24th, the squad-ron steamed for Man-il-a. Late on Sat-ur-day night, A-pril 30th, the ships en-tered the chan-nel lead-ing to Man-il-a Bay. No lights were shown on the ships, and the in-ten-tion was to try to pass the forts that guard the wide en-trance with-out be-ing seen. Sud-den-ly flames belched forth from the smoke-stack of the Mc-Cul-loch. The soot of the soft coal had caught fire from the in-tense heat of the fur-nace. A shot at once came from the forts. It was re-turned and the forts fired a-gain, but none of the shots hit, and the ships were soon out of range, un-harmed.

The squad-ron steamed on through the bay. It is sev-en-teen miles from the forts at the en-trance to Man-il-a, and as Com-mo-dore Dew-ey did not care to be-gin the fight till there was a clear light for his gun-ners to see the foe, the ships went at a slow rate of speed. The men were told to get what sleep they could, so that their nerves might be stead-y for the grim work they would have to do in the morn-ing. They lay down on the decks, stripped to the waist; guns, mag-a-zines, and am-mu-ni-tion hoists were read-y; the fur-na-ces blazed a-way, stor-ing up pow-er for the com-ing fray; and of-fi-cers moved a-bout, speak-ing in low tones, and see-ing that all things were in or-der. Just at day-break Man-il-a came in view. Man-y mer-chant ships were ly-ing in the har-bor, but no trace of the Span-ish fleet could yet be seen. The fleet steamed on to Cav-i-te, the na-val sta-tion, sev-en miles from Man-il-a, and here they found the ships they were in search of drawn up in a line in shal-low wa-ter.

The Span-iards be-gan the bat-tle, fire be-ing o-pened from the forts a-shore and from the ships at the same time. The Am-er-i-cans did not at once re-ply, but the ships moved slow-ly on in a line, the flag-ship, O-LYM-PI-A, in the lead, with Com-mo-dore Dew-ey him-self stand-ing on the for-ward bridge, at its most ex-posed place, to-ward the forts and the Span-ish ships. The BAL-TI-MORE, RA-LEIGH, PE-TREL, CON-CORD, and BOS-TON fol-lowed in the or-der named. When the O-LYM-PI-A had come with-in four thous-and yards of the Span-ish ships, she changed her course, and ran par-al-lel to the Span-ish line, the oth-er ships fol-low-ing her.

Then Com-mo-dore Dew-ey turned to Cap-tain Grid-ley of the O-LYM-PI-A, and said qui-et-ly, "Now you may fire, when read-y, Grid-ley."

The O-LYM-PI-A at once o-pened fire, and the oth-er ships fol-lowed, send-ing broad-side aft-er broad-side in-to the Span-ish ves-sels, with dead-ly aim, as they moved slow-ly past in line. Aft-er they had passed the ships of the foe, us-ing all the guns on the port side, they turned and re-passed, this time us-ing the star-board guns. Thus, while a con-stant fire was kept up, the men at the guns on one side had ten min-utes rest while those on the oth-er were at work. Five times our ships went

XVII.—THE BAT-TLE OF MAN-IL-A BAY.

back and forth in this way in front of the line of the foe, keep-ing up their pre-cise and de-struc-tive fire.

And all this time the Span-ish ships and forts were pour-ing forth shot and shell from ev-er-y gun. Tons and tons of i-ron and steel fell a-bout our ships, but so poor was their aim that but few struck—none to do great harm. At one time the REI-NA CHRIS-TI-NA, the flag-

THE O-LYM-PI-A AND THE REI-NA CHRIS-TI-NA.

ship of the Span-ish com-mand-er, Ad-mi-ral Mon-to-jo, came out to meet the O-LYM-PI-A. Ad-mi-ral Mon-to-jo, like Com-mo-dore Dew-ey, stood on the deck of his flagship, with his two sons as aides. The fire of all the O-LYM-PI-A's guns was at once turned on the REI-NA CHRIS-TI-NA, and a shot from one of them tore a-way one end of the bridge on which Ad-mi-ral Mon-to-jo stood. He stepped to the oth-er end, and kept on giv-ing or-ders to his gun crews. The two flag-ships had come with-in two thou-sand yards of each oth-er when the REI-NA CHRIS-TI-NA was forced by the aw-ful fire of the O-LYM-PI-A to turn back. As she swung round, a shell from the OLYM-PI-A struck her square-ly on the stern, un-der her pro-tec-tive deck, and ploughed through al-most her whole length, pier-cing her boil-ers, blow-ing up her for-ward mag-a-zine, and kill-ing her cap-tain and six-ty men. She was just a-ble to get back to shel-ter, and the fires start-ed in her were not put out till she sank.

At a-bout half past sev-en o'clock, some of the Span-ish ships be-ing sunk, and the fire from oth-ers hav-ing slack-ened, Com-mo-dore Dew-ey gave the sig-nal to stop fight-ing for a while. The men had been at their guns for two hours with on-ly a cup of cof-fee to keep them up, and the ships now drew off to the oth-er side of the bay, so that the crews might have their break-fast.

Soon aft-er e-lev-en o'clock, the fleet a-gain formed in

line, this time the BAL-TI-MORE in the lead. Fi-ring was re-sumed, and by half past twelve the Span-ish forts were si-lenced, and the ships all sunk, burnt, and de-sert-ed.

E-lev-en Span-ish war-ships, and two tor-pe-do boats were sunk or de-stroyed at Cav-i-te, twelve hun-dred Span-iards were killed or wound-ed, and Span-ish prop-er-ty to the val-ue of $6,000,000 had been de-stroyed or cap-tured. To bring these great re-sults to pass, Com-mo-dore Dew-ey had not had one man killed, and had on-ly eight slight-ly wound-ed. The dam-age done to his ships came on-ly to a-bout $5,000. No na-val bat-tle ev-er fought had end-ed with so clean and com-plete a vic-to-ry.

The next day Com-mo-dore Dew-ey oc-cu-pied the na-vy yard at Cav-i-te and drove the Span-ish force out. He cut the ca-ble, and set up a block-ade of Man-il-a. Hav-ing no land force, he con-tent-ed him-self with the con-trol of the bay of Man-il-a, while he wait-ed the com-ing of troops from the U-ni-ted States.

The news of his splen-did vic-to-ry was re-ceived with great joy in the U-ni-ted States, and with ad-mi-ra-tion and sur-prise all o-ver the world. No Am-er-i-can had feared that our na-vy would not keep up its cred-it and add to its fame, but so great a feat as this, a-chieved with-out the loss of a life, seemed like a mir-a-cle, and there was a grand out-burst of praise for Dew-ey and the brave and skill-ful tars on his ships. The Pres-i-dent raised him to the rank of rear ad-mi-ral, and Con-gress passed a res-o-lu-tion of thanks.

A-bout the time that Dew-ey was on his way to Man-il-a, a Span-ish fleet un-der the com-mand of Ad-mi-ral Cer-ve-ra, left the Cape Verde Isl-ands and steamed to the west-ward. The fleet con-sist-ed of four strong, swift, ar-mored cruis-ers, the best in Spain's na-vy, and three tor-pe-do-boat de-stroy-ers. As soon as it was known that they were on their way to this side, all our ships were on the a-lert to find out just where they meant to go. Ad-mi-ral Samp-son with part of his fleet cruised off the coast of Por-to Ri-co on the look-out for them, and a "fly-ing squad-ron," un-der com-mand of Com-mo-dore Schley was held at Hamp-ton Roads, to be read-y to go out and meet them in case they should come north and try to strike one of the coast cit-ies.

Some tim-id folks were in great fear all through this time, and tales of all sorts were fly-ing round that the Span-ish ships had been seen, now here, now there. At length, on May 14th, a re-port which turned out to be true came that they were at Mar-ti-nique, an isl-and far

Min-ne-ap-o-lis.   Tex-as.   Brook-lyn.   Mas-sa-chu-setts.   Co-lum-bi-a.
COM-MO-DORE SCHLEY'S FLY-ING SQUAD-RON.

to the south-east of Cu-ba. Com-mo-dore Schley's flying squad-ron at once got or-ders to go to Cu-ban wa-ters to help Ad-mi-ral Samp-son to find and whip the Span-ish fleet.

One of the Span-ish tor-pe-do-boat de-stroy-ers, the TER-ROR, was in need of re-pairs, and stayed at Mar-ti-nique when the rest of the fleet, af-ter a short stop, left there. They were next heard of at Cur-a-ca-o, an-o-ther isl-and off the South Am-er-i-can coast. Here they stopped on-ly long e-nough to take on coal and stores, and were then lost to sight for sev-er-al days. Com-mo-dore

Schley's squad-ron was or-dered to go to the south coast of Cu-ba to watch for them, while Ad-mi-ral Samp-son's fleet guard-ed the north coast.

On May 19th a re-port came from Spain that Cer-ve-ra's fleet had reached San-ti-a-go de Cu-ba, a port on the south coast of Cu-ba, but some doubt was felt as to the truth of this. It was thought that it might be on-ly a trick to throw our ships off the trail. The bay of San-ti-a-go has high hills all round it, has a ver-y nar-row mouth, guard-ed by strong forts, and is so long, and has such turns, that it is hard to see from the out-side what may be in it, so that it took some time to make sure that the Span-ish fleet was there. Com-mo-dore Schley brought all his ships to San-ti-a-go, and at length was a-ble to send word to Wash-ing-ton that he had Cer-ve-ra's fleet "bot-tled up," and he add-ed, "they will not get home."

Com-mo-dore Schley got or-ders not to seek a bat-tle with the Span-iards, but to keep up a block-ade of the port. Ad-mi-ral Samp-son, who had strong-er ships in his fleet, was or-dered to San-ti-a-go, and took charge of the block-ade. It was thought that so long as Cer-ve-ra's ships could be kept "bot-tled up" in the bay, there was no need to risk the loss of an-y of our ships by means of the mines and the forts in go-ing in to fight him.

But there was fear that in case of a storm at night, when our ships could not lie close to the shore, and, still more if there should be a fog, so that the search-lights would be of no use, there might be a chance for him to get out. So it was ver-y much to be wished that a "stopper" should be put in the "bot-tle," if a way could be found to do so.

The way to do it was found, and al-so the man to do it. On board with Ad-mi-ral Samp-son was a young of-fi-cer, Lieu-ten-ant Rich-mond Pear-son Hob-son. He was a na-val con-struct-or, but at his own re-quest had been al-lowed, when war broke out, to ex-change his du-ties in that line for ser-vice at sea. He pro-posed to Ad-mi-ral Samp-son to take a ves-sel in-to the mouth of the bay, and sink her at the point where there was least room, so that no ship could pass out. This plan meant al-most sure death for those who should try to car-ry it out, but Hob-son said that six men could do it, and he of-fered to lead them him-self.

The plan was ap-proved by Ad-mi-ral Samp-son, and the coll-ier MER-RI-MAC was picked out as the best boat to use. Vol-un-teers were called for, and sev-er-al hun-dred of the men of-fered to go. When a choice of six was made, man-y of those not ta-ken shed tears be-cause they could not have the chance to take part in this per-il-ous but glo-ri-ous un-der-ta-king.

Just be-fore three o'clock, on Fri-day morn-ing, June 3d, Hob-son set out with his brave crew. He had sev-en men with him, for one be-sides the cho-sen six stowed him-self on board. A Span-ish pick-et-boat saw the MER-RI-MAC as soon as she poked her nose in the chan-nel and gave the a-larm. In a mo-ment the guns of the forts on each side, and of some of the war-ships, were turned on her. Mines and tor-pe-does went off on all sides. One shot took a-way the MER-RI-MAC's rud-der, and this spoiled part of the scheme, for they could not turn her a-cross the chan-nel. As soon as she was in the right place, they cast her an-chors, and some of the men launched a cat-a-ma-ran on which they were to try to escape. Then Hob-son touched off the ex-plo-sives on board. The ship was lift-ed al-most out of the wa-ter, and then set-tled back and be-gan to sink. The men had scram-bled on to the cat-a-ma-ran, and start-ed to get out of the bay. But a strong tide was run-ning, and day-light came and found them still strug-gling in the wa-ter. The Span-iards then saw them, and sent a boat to pick them up.

In the mean time, those on the ships out-side were

OUR NAVAL HEROES.

HOB-SON AND HIS MEN LEAV-ING THE MER-RI-MAC.

watch-ing for them with anx-ious eyes; but as time passed, and no sign of them was seen, there be-gan to be small hope that an-y had es-caped. In the course of the fore-noon, how-ev-er, a Span-ish boat came out with a flag of truce. Ad-mi-ral Cer-ve-ra's chief-of-staff was in the boat, and he brought to Ad-mi-ral Samp-son this mes-sage from the Span-ish com-mand-er: "Your boys will be all right in our hands. Dar-ing like theirs makes the bit-ter-est en-e-my proud that his fel-low men can be such he-roes. .... They are our pris-on-ers, but our friends. Ev-er-y-thing is be-ing done to make their stay with us com-fort-a-ble. If you wish to send them an-y-thing, we will cheer-ful-ly take it to them."

Hob-son and his men were held as pris-on-ers for thir-ty-three days be-fore they could be re-leased by an ex-change. When the young he-ro came back to the U-ni-ted States, he found the whole coun-try ring-ing with his praise, and crowds fol-lowed and cheered him wher-ev-er he went. Ev-er-y one e-choed the say-ing of Ad-mi-ral Samp-son that "a bra-ver deed had not been done since Cush-ing blew up the AL-BE-MARLE."

Hob-son came from Geor-gi-a, one of the States of the South, and ma-ny oth-ers from that part of the land did brave deeds in this war, side by side with the men from the North. This was a thing that all were glad to see, for it was a clear sign that all the ill-will of the Civ-il War had died out, and that those who had once met as brave foes were now good friends, with one flag, and one coun-try.

A num-ber of plans for in-va-ding Cu-ba had been talked of, but none a-dopt-ed as yet, on ac-count of the un-cer-tain-ty a-bout the Span-ish fleet. This be-ing now at an end, it was de-ci-ded to land an ar-my near San-ti-a-go, to be-siege the town, and cap-ture or de-stroy the ships from the land side. In the mean-while, our fleet kept watch out-side, read-y to join in the bom-bard-ment as soon as the troops were in place. It has al-read-y been said that the shoot-ing a-way of the MER-RI-MAC's rud-der had pre-vent-ed her from be-ing placed a-cross the mouth of the bay so as whol-ly to block it. The Span-iards found that, with care, a ship might steer its way past the wreck, and, when our troops be-gan to press the siege of San-ti-a-go, Ad-mi-ral Cer-ve-ra got or-ders to go out and face our fleet, and try to get a-way if he could. He chose Sun-day morn-ing, Ju-ly 3d, for the at-tempt.

The men on our ships in front of the port were at Sun-day "quar-ters for in-spec-tion," when, at a-bout 9.35 A. M., a mass of smoke was seen go-ing be-hind the hills which shut in the bay, and soon a Span-ish war-ship came tear-ing out at full speed. A sig-nal was made from more than one of our ships at the same time, "En-em-y's ships es-ca-ping," and the com-mand, "All hands clear for ac-tion," rang out. The men cheered as they sprang to their guns, and fire was o-pened at once by the ships near-est the mouth of the bay. The IN-FAN-TA MA-RI-A TER-E-SA, Ad-mi-ral Cer-ve-ra's flag-ship, lead the Span-ish fleet, and the VIZ-CA-YA, CRIS-TO-BAL CO-LON, AL-MI-RAN-TE O-QUEN-DO, and the tor-pe-do-boat de-stroy-ers FU-ROR and PLU-TON, fol-lowed. They came fi-ring all guns, and dense smoke at once spread o-ver the wa-ter, and the noise of the ex-plo-sions be-came one long roar. Our ships were spread out in a long line stretch-ing both ways from the mouth of the bay, and as the Span-ish fleet turned to the west, the task of fight-ing and cha-sing them fell chief-ly to the ships at that end of the line, which were the OR-E-GON, the I-O-WA, the TEX-AS, and the BROOK-LYN. The splen-did gun-ner-y which our men had shown at Man-il-a was re-peat-ed by those here, and two of the Span-ish ships, the MA-RI-A TER-E-SA and the O-QUEN-DO, were soon so dam-aged that they had to run for the beach, where they were burnt and blown up. The VIZ-CA-YA and the CO-LON kept on at full speed to the west-ward, and a run-ning fight be-tween them and our ships went on for near-ly an hour, when the VIZ-CA-YA took fire, and was al-so turned to the shore and run a-ground. The CO-LON had still a

XVIII.—DESTRUCTION OF CERVERA'S FLEET AT SANTIAGO DE CUBA.

good lead, and for a while it looked as if she might escape. But the BROOK-LYN and OR-E-GON fol-lowed, keep-ing up a ter-rif-ic fire, and slow-ly catch-ing up with their prey; the OR-E-GON, in par-tic-u-lar, show-ing her-self to be a won-der of speed for so heav-y a bat-tle-ship. By de-grees, the CO-LON was forced in-shore, and at 1.20 P. M., at a point for-ty-eight miles from the mouth of San-ti-a-go Bay, she ran on to the beach, and hauled down her flag.

The two de-stroy-ers, FU-ROR and PLU-TON, had been done for ear-ly in the fight, their ca-reer hav-ing come to an end with-in twen-ty min-utes from the time they came out of the bay. They re-ceived much dam-age from the fire of the IN-DI-AN-A, I-O-WA, and TEX-AS, but the lar-gest share of the work in their de-struc-tion was done by the lit-tle GLOU-CES-TER, a yacht that had been turned in-to a war-ship. She got be-tween them, and pound-ed a-way mad-ly at close range with her small guns at both of them. They sunk with-in a few min-utes of each-oth-er, and few of the crews of ei-ther were left a-live.

The re-sult of the morn-ing's work was the de-struc-tion of the Span-ish fleet, and the cap-ture of the Ad-mi-ral and a-bout fif-teen hun-dred pris-on-ers, with a loss to the Span-ish of some six hun-dred men killed.

THE GLOU-CES-TER DE-STROY-ING THE FU-ROR AND PLU-TON.

On the Am-er-i-can side, one man was killed, and one wound-ed, both on the BROOK-LYN. Sev-er-al of the ships were struck, the BROOK-LYN more of-ten than the oth-ers, but in all the dam-age was won-der-ful-ly small.

The skill and bra-ver-y shown by the Am-er-i-can tars in the fight, was hard-ly more re-mark-a-ble than the gal-lant spir-it they dis-played in sa-ving the Span-ish crews from the wrecked and burn-ing ships as soon as they sur-ren-dered. The task was one of no small dan-ger. Guns left load-ed were send-ing their shots on all sides, and mag-a-zines were blow-ing up as the flames came near them. The decks were hot, and the wrecks full of smoke. But no risk kept our men from try-ing to save all that could be reached. Ad-mi-ral Cer-ve-ra was a-mong the res-cued, and when he came on board the I-o-wa he got a hear-ty cheer from the crew. What Cap-tain Ev-ans, of that ship, said of his men, ap-plied with as much truth to all the oth-er crews: "So long as the en-e-my showed his flag, they fought like Am-er-i-can sea-men, but when the flag came down, they were as gen-tle and ten-der as Am-er-i-can wom-en."

Spain's na-val pow-er on this side of the At-lan-tic was now at an end. She still had a fleet, un-der com-mand of Ad-mi-ral Cam-a-ra, which, aft-er sail-ing on June 16th from Ca-diz, had gone through the Med-i-ter-ra-ne-an Sea and the Su-ez Can-al, on its way eith-er to Man-il-a or our Pa-cif-ic coast. But as soon as our gov-ern-ment an-nounced that it meant to send a fleet to strike the coast of Spain it-self, Ad-mi-ral Cam-a-ra was or-dered to come back home. Ac-tive pre-par-a-tions for the des-patch of our fleet a-cross the At-lan-tic went on through the first weeks of Ju-ly, but this pro-ject did not need to be car-ried out. The sur-ren-der of San-ti-a-go and all the Span-ish troops in the east end of Cu-ba took place Ju-ly 17th, and this, fol-low-ing the smash-ing of Cer-ve-ra's fleet, seemed to make it plain to the Span-ish gov-ern-ment that the time had come to cry "e-nough." On Ju-ly 26th, the French am-bas-sa-dor, on be-half of Spain, asked for our terms of peace, and the ne-go-ti-a-tions thus be-gun led to the sign-ing, on Au-gust 12th, of a pro-to-col which put a stop to ac-tive war.

The terms a-greed to by Spain in the pro-to-col in-clu-ded the giv-ing up of all claim to Cu-ba, and the ces-sion to the U-ni-ted States of Por-to Ri-co and oth-er Span-ish isl-ands in the West In-dies. Each of the two gov-ern-ments were to ap-point com-mis-sion-ers to meet at Par-is, and ar-range a trea-ty of peace, in which all the de-tails should be fixed.

These com-mis-sion-ers met in due course, and, aft-er long de-bate, made a fi-nal set-tle-ment. In this, Spain, be-sides what she had al-read-y yield-ed, gave up to the U-ni-ted States the con-trol of the Phil-ip-pine Isl-ands; the U-ni-ted States a-gree-ing to pay her, by way of com-pen-sa-tion, the sum of $20,000,000.

CPSIA information can be obtained
at www.ICGtesting.com
Printed in the USA
LVHW031251151221
706194LV00004B/274